RAYMOND BAXTER'S
FARNBOROUGH
COMMENTARY

Good luck!

Raymond Baxter

RAYMOND BAXTER'S
FARNBOROUGH
COMMENTARY

Foreword by John Cunningham

PSL Patrick Stephens, Cambridge

Dedication To the pilots.

Text © Raymond Baxter 1980

First published in 1980

British Cataloguing in Publication Data

Baxter, Raymond
   Raymond Baxter's Farnborough commentary.
   1. Farnborough Air Display—History
   I. Farnborough commentary
   629.1'074'0422725   TL506.G72F/

   ISBN 0-85059-434-0

Photoset in 10 on 10pt Baskerville type
by Manuset Limited, Baldock, Herts.
Printed and bound in Great Britain on
Huntsman Velvet 120 gsm coated cartridge
by The Garden City Press, Letchworth, Herts,
for the publishers, Patrick Stephens Limited,
Bar Hill, Cambridge, CB3 8EL, England

Title pages *Concorde's long-awaited first appearance thrills the Farnborough crowds.*

Front endpaper *Flashback to the days when aircraft still stood 'tail down'—Farnborough in 1948.*

Back endpaper *The static park in 1960 when great names still retained their individuality.*

Contents

Acknowledgements

Whatever it is, this book is certainly not what the publisher had in mind when he first approached me. I am therefore indebted for his tolerance. I am also greatly obliged for their generous response to my appeal for pictures to Robert Gardner, Darby Childerhouse and their colleagues of British Aerospace and its component companies. My thanks for their photographs also go to Michael J.F. Bowyer, the Ministry of Defence, Colin Riach of the BBC, Peter Guiver and Bruce Robertson. Reference to back-numbers of *Flight* and *The Aeroplane* has been invaluable as has Charles Simms' book *Farnborough Highlights*.

I am also indebted to Chris Wren for his historic cartoon, John Blake for his limerick and drawing and to A.W. 'Bill' Bedford, OBE, AFC, FRAeS, for agreeing to read the manuscript. He took it with him on a flight to Bangkok during which it was 'christened' in champagne, within sight, I am told, of Mount Everest. Those of his noted comments which survived and were printable were as encouraging as they were pertinent. Finally, I would like to thank Bruce Quarrie for editing my manuscript and John Cunningham for providing such a generous Foreword.

An attempt to condense into a few thousand words the impressions of 30 years will inevitably incur omissions. To all those not mentioned who ought to have been, my apologies. Next time perhaps?

Foreword

Group Captain John Cunningham,CBE,DSO**,DFC*,DL,FRAeS

Raymond Baxter has taken part in all the SBAC Farnborough displays for the last thirty years as a commentator and on many occasions flown in some of the aircraft being displayed. In this book he has captured much of the spirit of what has perhaps been one of the most exciting times in aviation development.

Those of us who had the privilege of taking part in these displays look back on the late 1940s and 1950-60 as a time when a large number of new types of aircraft were being built and pilots were learning how to display them effectively. Inevitably, there was rivalry between the different British companies but equally there was a very happy relationship between the pilots.

In the last ten years we have seen some very high performance aircraft demonstrated and inevitably the form of the demonstration becomes somewhat stereotyped, but the positioning and judgement required of the pilot to give his display over the airfield, and in sight of the crowd, is of a very high order.

Probably the Harrier has caught the eye more than any other aircraft in recent years and Raymond Baxter gives a good account of its astonishing capabilities.

I commend this book as it gives a well-illustrated history of many of the aircraft and pilots who have performed at the Display during the last thirty years.

Hatfield, 1980

Introduction

For as long as I can remember I have been in love with aeroplanes. A favourite uncle, with whom I was spending a weekend, took me as a very little boy to Croydon Aerodrome. It must have been in the late '20s. London's airport, together with the Lyceum Pantomime, were the most exciting things that had ever happened to me. It was dusk when we arrived and to this day I can see the silhouettes of the great biplane airliners trundling across the grass towards the control tower to disembark their elegant passengers, while men in smart blue uniforms saluted. The very name Imperial Airways made my tummy tingle inexplicably.

One of the major traumatic experiences of my childhood was missing the school excursion to the Hendon Air Display of 1932. I was rushed to hospital with appendicitis and nearly died of disappointment.

Later, as 13-year-olds, my best friend and I cycled from my paternal grandmother's birthplace, the Essex village of Little Chesterford, to the RAF airfield at Duxford. There we watched spellbound for hours the beautiful Gauntlets and Gladiators, and secretly I knew that what I wanted most in the world was to fly aeroplanes like that.

My father was a man of remarkable perception and from him I learned as early as 1936 that the tragedy of another war with Germany appeared inevitable.

In that year Alan Cobham's Flying Circus came to Fairlop, a disused First World War airfield some ten miles from our home, I took a ten shilling note and six pence from my money box and without a word to anyone cycled off alone to meet my destiny.

'You're 16 of course, aren't you lad?' said the man in the pay-box.

'Yes sir' I lied, as I handed him nearly six months' pocket-money.

The ten or fifteen minutes which followed could have been as many years or seconds. They have assumed the dream-like quality of a great symphony. I remember looking down vertically at the earth below. Did the God-like figure in the leather flying coat and helmet loop me on my first flight? I shall never know.

As we skimmed over the hedge to land—so unbelievably fast and so close to the ground—I remember thinking 'How can I ever make myself clever and brave enough to do this?'

I cycled home still in my dream, and in response to my parent's casual enquiry 'And where have you been, may I ask?' I said 'I've been flying Father. And when the war comes, that's what I'm going to do.' He turned away for a moment, and then he put his arm across my shoulders, and he said 'Then I can only wish you luck, my son—but I hope to Heaven you may never have to do it.' At that moment I am sure he knew, and I knew, that I would.

So at $17\frac{3}{4}$, as soon as I was old enough, I signed the forms, became a Spitfire pilot, and by the Grace of God, lived happily ever after.

Until now I have told that story only to my family. I write it here merely to indicate my remarkable good fortune in having been actually paid by the BBC to attend, amongst other aviation occasions, every Farnborough Air Display since 1950. Some consolation, you may think, for missing that school outing to Hendon in 1932. But it still rankles.

Raymond Baxter

Denham, Bucks, 1980

In the beginning

Farnborough in Hampshire has as good a claim as anywhere to call itself the cradle of British aviation.

As early as the turn of the century, the strange goings-on at Laffans Plain were the gossip of those delightful pubs which to this day, adorn the wooded heathland on the Surrey border. The surrounding Crown land had long been Army country. The first unit of Britain's fighting forces to be dedicated solely to aviation, the Air Battalion of the Royal Engineers, was formed and based there. In 1905 it was chosen as the site for the Government Balloon Factory. But so rapidly was the heavier-than-air concept gaining ground that six years later it was re-named the Army Aircraft Factory; later the Royal Aircraft Factory.

During the First World War amongst its contributions was the design and construction of the immortal SE5 biplane fighter. In 1918 it became, and remains to this day, the Royal Aircraft Establishment. Over the years its record of technological achievement is unrivalled by a single institution anywhere in the world.

To the visitor of any sensibility the place is heady with atmosphere. Many of the original buildings still stand in the unplanned maze which has sprung up around the original site. The old Black Sheds became a landmark familiar throughout the aviation world. Curious wisps of steam and extraordinary shapes add a touch of slightly sinister fantasy. Security, real or imagined, is an evident preoccupation. One has the feeling of being simultaneously in the past, the present and the future.

Above left 'Cowboy' Cody and one of his man-lifting kites at Farnborough in 1906. **Left** The Cody Aeroplane, a development of the first Cody biplane of 1908, which was known as British Military Aeroplane No 1. All Cody's aeroplane work was done at Farnborough. From the airfield there, on October 5 1908, he made the first official aeroplane flight in Great Britain, achieving a distance of 496 yards.

Take Cody's Tree for example. These vestigial remains of some long-dead specimen are carefully preserved against further ruin. They mark the supposed starting point of the first flight of an all-British aeroplane. Samuel Cody gave it his name. An American-born expert on man-lifting kites, he was under contract to the War Office. Growing more adventurous he built an ungainly machine called the "Cathedral". It killed him on take-off in 1913.

Others were more successful. The arrival of Geoffrey de Havilland from his first base at Newbury increased Farnborough's capability and importance. It is typical of the price of progress in aviation that some 30 years and two World Wars later, Sir Geoffrey's eldest son was killed in 1946 flying his experimental high speed jet, the DH 108. In September 1948 the 108 became the first British aircraft officially to exceed the speed of sound. The pilot was John Derry.

Typical too of the triumphs and tragedies of the industry is the story of its own 'Society of British Aircraft Constructors', formed in 1916. In 1960 a spate of Government-inspired mergers created the British Aircraft Corporation on the one hand, and the Hawker Siddeley Group on the other. Farnborough wags promptly dubbed the SBAC the 'Society of Both Aircraft Constructors'. Today it is the Society of British Aerospace Companies.

Back in the '30s it was surprisingly slow to jump on to the band-wagon set rolling by the great RAF Air Days at Hendon. These astonishing displays were the brainchild of the father of the Royal Air Force, Lord Trenchard. His primary purpose was to show off his spirited offspring to John Citizen who was paying for it. The first of these Air Pageants was staged in 1920 and its instant success led to a series of annual events.

But not until 1932 did the SBAC organise the addition of further aircraft to a glorified trade show at Hendon on the day following the RAF Display. In

Above left *Geoffrey de Havilland, pioneer pilot, designer and father figure of British aviation.* **Above right** *A military balloon, circa 1890. Balloons such as this were produced by the Establishment in the last two decades of the 19th century under the direction of Colonel J.L.B. Templer and Colonel J.E. Capper. The envelopes were usually constructed of goldbeaters' skin.*

his excellent book *Farnborough*, Charles Simms notes that cameras were not allowed. As the leading aviation photographer of his day my old friend may be forgiven for recording, forty years later, his resentment of this curious imposition. It was not only absurd but pathetic since every machine displayed had already been described in meticulous detail in *Flight* and *The Aeroplane*, not least by Simms himself.

Curiously enough I too have experience of the SBAC's arcane attitude towards 'security'. When in 1974 a USAF Lockheed SR71 'Blackbird' flew into the Farnborough Show direct from California and supersonic all the way (NY—London 1 hour 55 minutes) my request for a television interview with the record-breaking crew on their arrival was peremptorily refused. In reply to my protests I was actually denied admittance to the airfield. We got our interview as the crew disembarked, and the Americans needless to say, could not have been more helpful and charming. Was that not after all precisely why they had come? But it really was all rather silly and annoying at the time.

Immediately after the Second World War, the SBAC cast its mind back to the successes of Hendon 1932-35 and Hatfield 1936-7. To their great credit they got their show back on the road as early as September 12 1946. The Handley Page airfield and factory at Radlett in Hertfordshire was the chosen site, and a return visit was made the following year.

It was not until 1948 that the move was made to Farnborough where the amount of space available—not least to the ever growing crowds of spectators and their cars—ensured the increasing scope and success of the show.

I returned from my first broadcasting job with the British Forces Network based in Hamburg in the summer of 1949. Naturally I made a point of listening to Charles Gardner's radio commentary from Farnborough, as I had in Germany the previous year. Perhaps in my wildest dreams I entertained the idea of being there myself one day. □

Above *Cody's Own outside the Farnborough shed in which it was built. It crashed on take-off.* **Below** *Beautiful original—the high-speed SE4 photographed at Farnborough on June 17 1914 with the airship, administration and aircraft buildings in the background.*

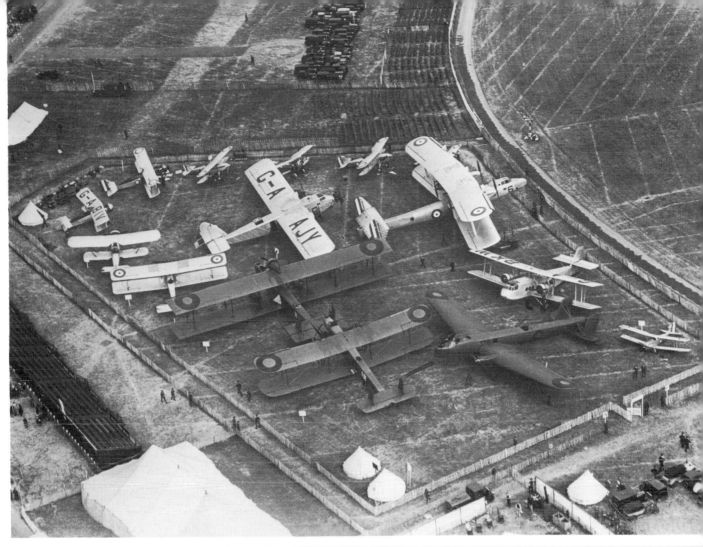

Above left *Designed at Farnborough in 1916, a current example of the SE5a rebuilt and refurbished by apprentices and maintained at Farnborough in flying condition over 60 years later*

Left *Early smoke signals—Grebes at Hendon in 1930.*

Above *In the beginning—the New Types park at Hendon in 1932.*

Right *DH 108 Swallow, flown at Farnborough in 1946 by Geoffrey de Havilland, one of the 'few' who gave their lives in pursuit of supersonic safety. Flown by John Derry, the DH 108 was the first British aircraft officially to exceed the speed of sound in September 1948.*

Above *The SR71 Blackbird dwarfed by the tail of its US 'big brother' Galaxy in 1974* **Below** *The Lysander's debut at the last Hendon display in 1937.* **Opposite page** *Handley Page Hermes, which first appeared at Radlett in 1947, following the Hastings of the previous year. The first prototype crashed on its initial take-off. The original Bristol Hercules engines were replaced by four Rolls Royce Merlins.*

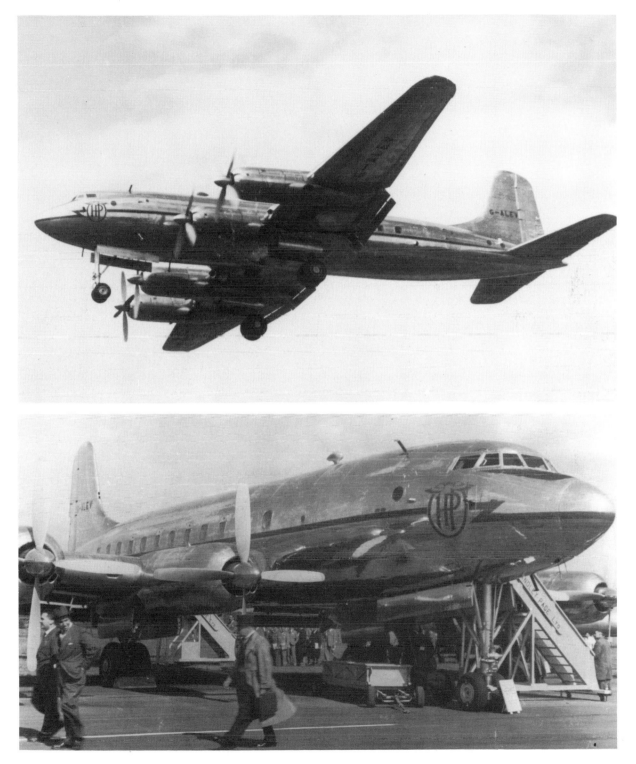

Vintage years

When Malcolm Muggeridge was editor of *Punch* a literary lady silenced the shrill chatter of a Bloomsbury cocktail party by thundering at him accusingly, 'Mr Muggeridge, *Punch* is not what it was!'

'No ma'am', replied the sage, 'But then it never was, was it?'

It is a temptation of age to compare unfavourably the present with the past. But who having enjoyed them could deny that the 1950s were the vintage years of the Farnborough Air Display?

The British aircraft industry was redolent with the confidence born of its wartime triumphs. Developments of the great piston engined fighting aeroplanes promised continued success for a further generation. Far more important and exciting was the challenging leap forward into the jet age. Had not the Gloster Whittle shown the way as early as

May 1941? The Meteor, its direct descendant and the Allies' first combat jet, entered squadron service with the RAF in July 1944, and de Havilland had swiftly followed with the Vampire which first flew in September 1943 and was squadron equipment by December 1945. Few Britons questioned that the world's finest aircraft were built in this country, that they would continue to be so in the foreseeable future, and that the American aviation industry had better look to its laurels if it hoped to retain a share of the liberated markets of our brave new post-war world.

The attitudes of those days may seem curiously chauvinistic and complacent by modern standards. But we had won the war hadn't we?—and the men who had designed, built and flown the aircraft which destroyed the Luftwaffe turned to their peacetime aviation pursuits with the zest and enthusiasm

born of the years of struggle. This was particularly true of the pilots. The Empire Test Pilots School was at Farnborough itself, and until well into the '60s the ETP Mess was the social hub of the flying world during the week of the Display. Wild and uproarious were some of the parties held there. For many it was a glimpse back to the rip-roaring squadron life in which they had so recently grown up, and 'a booze up with the boys' was not then regarded in any way untoward behaviour for a professional test pilot, as it would be today.

Incredible as it may now seem, as show after show produced its prototypes groping their way towards supersonic flight, an unofficial competition to produce the best 'sonic boom' of the Display flourished amongst the test pilots for several years, and was itself a major attraction to the crowds.

In those days the principal Public Address commentator was Oliver Stewart—a man always credited in print with the rank of Major, and a very military figure. He broadcast to the crowd from the open flat roof of the control tower, and Farnborough weather being then much as it is today, as often as not he would be seen wearing a huge cavalry waterproof heavily hung with buckles and straps.

To this day I can see him literally stamping his feet with excitement while his commentary rose to the pitch of near hysteria as Neville Duke, or Mike Lithgow or John Derry hurtled down from altitude to penetrate 'The Sound Barrier', and seconds later

appeared in a screaming pass along the runway display line.

I was there as very much a junior to the then BBC Air Correspondent, Charles Gardner, who surely contributed as much as any in his day towards making Britain air-minded. Gardner left the staff of the BBC in 1953 to join Sir George Edwards' team at Vickers, retiring as head of the British Aircraft Corporation's publicity machine on the very day of Nationalisation of the aircraft industry, June 29 1977. He must have been the first to broadcast a running commentary on a genuine aerial dog-fight—seen from the Dover cliffs early in the Battle of Britain. Subsequently he himself became an RAF pilot, flying Catalinas with 240 and 205 Squadrons. He was far and away the best all-round air correspondent the BBC ever had, and I make no bones of the fact that I owe him much—not merely from my fledgling days as a broadcaster, but in a long professional association during which we became personal friends.

Even before leaving the BBC Charles Gardner was responsible for much of the Farnborough PA commentary, taking over completely when Oliver Stewart retired, and continuing until 1974. It is a sad reflection on the SBAC that no official of that august body sent him so much as a postcard of thanks after more than 25 years of unstinting professionalism in the task of keeping the crowds informed. Happily the omission was eventually, and properly, rectified.

Phrases he employed in both his closed circuit

Left *Sapphire Meteor in 1950.*

Right *Charles Gardner and Oliver Stewart in the commentary box on the roof of the control tower.*

Far right *Early mentor—Charles Gardner and myself with the prototype Valiant.*

and BBC broadcasts are still fresh in my memory:

'The great triumvirate of V Bombers—the Valiant, Vulcan and Victor, joined by their three civil counterparts, the incomparable Comet, the Britannia and the Viscount, demonstrating to the world the position of leadership won the hard way by the British aviation industry.'

There was a ring to his words which captured the heady atmosphere of confidence so soon to be undermined by political miscalculation, financial mismanagement, strikes and go-slows—and indeed perhaps, by its own complacency.

Certainly there was ample technical achievement to justify optimism in the shape, literally, of things to come. The Avro 707B first flew on September 6 1950 and appeared at Farnborough the following day. Its delta wing typified then unfamiliar and exciting concepts pursued in a decade of single-

Above left *Sir Alan Cobham was a world pioneer of in-flight refuelling, forming a private company to prove his point. This shows an early demonstration in 1950 using a Lincoln and a Meteor.* **Left** *A rare bird, the Avro Ashton—jet powered version of the ill-fated Tudor—in 1951.* **Below** *De Havilland quartet—Vampires and Comet in 1949.* **Right** *Flight refuelling is thirsty work—here a Victor tanker of 55 Squadron refuels two Lightnings of No 5 Squadron in 1968.*

seater experimental prototypes. In 1953 Avro staged an all-delta flypast of six aircraft—two Vulcans and four 707s.

Another delta was the Boulton Paul P111 which had removable wing and tail tips to facilitate research. The Short SB5 of 1953 offered three alternative angles of wing-sweep—50°, 60° and 69°—although this foretaste of the F-111 and Tornado 'variable geometry' was as yet a hangar job, not an airborne option.

The elegant little Fairey Delta 2 was, contrary to popular belief across the Atlantic, the world's first aircraft to establish an official speed record in excess of 1,000 mph. Flown by Peter Twiss, it achieved 1,132 mph on March 10 1956.

Of the larger airframes of the period comment will be made in a later chapter, but let no-one assume that the glamour and confidence of the '50s was confined to a handful of experimental prototypes. The original Gloster Javelin first flew in November 1951, appearing at Farnborough the following September flown by Bill Waterton. In the 1954 Display five Javelins executed a formation fly-past, and the aircraft was in squadron service by 1956—and that had been an unusual-enough shape when it first appeared.

Even more remarkable was the progress of the

Hawker Hunter as seen in successive Displays. First flown in June 1951, it made its Farnborough debut in '52, and the following year Neville Duke flew in immediately after establishing a new World Air Speed Record at 727.6 mph. In the hands of a team of test pilots which included Bill Bedford, Hugh Merewether, Duncan Simpson, David Lockspeiser and Frank Bullen, as well as Neville Duke, the Hunter could not have been better displayed. Even more remarkable, as early as 1955 we saw no less than 64 Hunters from Fighter Command in a 400-knot formation fly-past at 1,500 feet, and three years later the unforgettable low level loop by 22 Hunters from Treble One Squadron, led by Squadron Leader Roger Topp.

Farnborough presented a visible record of the achievements of Britain's outstanding post-war success in fighting aeroplanes. 1,972 Hunters had been built by the final delivery—a T7 in July 1954—and there is no shadow of doubt that at least a further 1,500 could have been sold had production not been terminated so absurdly prematurely. No fewer than 510, refurbished at the factory, found ready purchasers 'second-hand' all over the world and the Hunter was still an attractive proposition more than 20 years after production was ceased.

A further touch of romance was added to the '50s

Top *The Victor B1 prototype photographed in 1953.* **Above and below** *Seen at Farnborough during 1944-45 but never displayed to the public—a captured Luftwaffe Heinkel He 177 and Dornier Do 335.*

by the renewal of the old rivalry between Hawker and Supermarine, as exemplified by the Hurricane and Spitfire. Neville Duke's Hunter record of '53 was broken the following year by Mike 'Lucky' Lithgow in a Swift F4, although he had to seek the warmer air of Tripoli to notch up an extra 10 mph. Backed up by Dave Morgan, Lithgow's displays of the Swift variants which followed the Supermarine 510 and 535 prototypes, and the twin naval 525, kept their Hawker Siddeley rivals on their mettle. Meantime Roland Beamont's Canberras and P1, Peter Twiss with the FD1 and 2, Ted Tennant's Folland Midge (forerunner of the Gnat), and the amazing former Gloster test pilot Jan Zurakowski with the ungainly-looking Avro Canada CF-100, were giving the crowds, and the connoisseurs, exhibitions of display aerobatics the like of which had never previously been possible.

Nor was it only the fixed wing aircraft which were breaking new ground. Charles 'Sox' Hosegood, with whom I had made a series of radio programmes about helicopter-flying and its potential applications, brought the twin-rotor stub-winged Bristol 173 to the Display in 1953 and '54, looking for all the world like a flying tube-train. Redesigned as the 192 it appeared again in 1959—the year of the first appearance of the SRN1 hovercraft which, blowing up clouds of newly cut grass, was described by resident wags as the world's fastest lawn mower. Saunders-Roe's Chief Test Pilot Peter Lamb was at the controls with a load of fully armed Royal Marines littering his 'decks', hugely enjoying their unconventional ride while becoming the world's first hovercraft passengers.

Another amazing machine of that year, in which I also had a ride, was the Fairey Rotodyne. Part helicopter, part autogyro, it was claimed to be the world's first vertical take-off airliner. Powered by two Napier Elands it enjoyed direct rotor-drive by means of rotor-tip jets; was ordered for commuter service in the US; was years ahead of its time but never emerged from the prototype stage, not least because of insuperable noise problems at the hover.

But it was primarily the intense excitement and fierce rivalry of those early years of trans-sonic flight which made the decade so unforgettable. Designers and pilots were pushing at the frontiers of their knowledge, and in this lay the roots of the most tragic disaster ever to mar the Farnborough Display. I have never ceased to thank my stars that I did not see it. In fact I was driving home when I heard the news on my car radio. It was during the Saturday public show in 1952. Having completed my broadcasting commitments and watched the show throughout the week, I left the airfield some 40 minutes before the end of the Display to avoid the traffic jams. It was estimated that the record crowd exceeded 140,000 people. John Derry was flying de Havilland's successor to the Vampire and 108, the DH 110 in the unofficial high-speed stakes. After his dive from altitude to generate the anticipated sonic boom, he pulled out and was turning behind the control tower when the aircraft started to break up. One of the engines fell into the crowd not far from the hill, causing death and injury to spectators. John Derry and his flight-test observer Tony Richards were both killed.

Within minutes Neville Duke was continuing the Display with his own spectacular booming dive, precisely as John Derry would have wished and

Below *Vickers Valiant—the first of the great triumvirate of British V-bombers. They were of historic importance in giving credibility to Britain's independent nuclear deterrent. Jock Bryce took the Valiant off at its Farnborough debut in 1951 in a near-vertical climb—an example of showmanship worthy of his skill as a totally dedicated company test pilot with whom it was my good fortune to fly on several occasions.*

expected. I am sure too that Derry would have wished for no finer epitaph than that by common consent of colleagues and their successors his name was given to the roll-under turn which was one of the hallmarks of his unfailingly excellent display flying.

In more material form, what finer memorial could there have been to this brilliant test pilot than that the DH 110, developed into the Sea Vixen, should have appeared at Farnborough six years after his death as a production aircraft for the Royal Navy?

One further comment is required in any review of British Aviation in the '50s. Brief mention has been made of 'Bea' Beaumont's appearance with the English Electric P1. Its predecessor for research and development was the prototype Short SB5. The aim of its designer, 'Teddy' Petter, the creator of the Canberra, was to produce the first RAF fighter capable of exceeding Mach 1 in straight and level flight. The P1 was known to exist in 1954 but allegedly for reasons of security it was prohibited from displaying at Farnborough. Roland Beamont recalls that this annoyed him so much that flying in the vicinity at 40,000 feet he was seriously tempted to 'drop in' on the show unheralded and unannounced.

The following year he was permitted to display, but frustrated by performance restrictions, he was unable to 'out-bang' his contemporaries in the manner well within his grasp.

The career of what was to become the Lightning was subsequently further bedevilled by that classic political miscalculation, the Defence White Paper of April 1957. This categorically declared the obsolesence of manned fighters for the Royal Air Force—a policy decision presided over by Duncan Sandys, and greeted by not a single resignation from the Air Council. Mercifully 20 prototypes had been commissioned, and re-engined with two RR Avons, Mach 2 was achieved in November 1958, and two years later the Lightning F1 was cleared for service. Not until 1964 was the absurdity of the White Paper officially rescinded in the commissioning of the vastly improved Mk 3 and BAC's long ignored advice to double the fuel capacity was finally accepted the following year.

More than 20 years later, thanks to the Lightning's extended service, together with that of the Phantoms, Britain's air defence has been made narrowly viable during the dangerous interim awaiting the arrival of the ADR version of Tornado. But what a sad contrast is written between the adventurous confidence of the early '50s and the confusion and ineptitude which marred the end of the decade. As much as the ruthless and unrelenting competition of the US aircraft industry and its world wide political lobby, Denis Healey's cancellation of TSR2 and the half-hearted approach of successive British Governments and their servants to supersonics, VTOL and other trail-blazing projects cost this country the world leadership which **was once within its grasp.**   □

Below left *Bristol Britannia photographed in 1952.* **Above** *The Comet 1 prototype in 1950. Arnold Hall, then Director RAE, headed the pre-disaster Comet research programme. For this and his other services to British aviation he was knighted.* **Below** *Airborne early warning Comet—prototype for production AEW Nimrod—a sophisticated descendant of the original aircraft a quarter century earlier.*

Above *The incomparable Vulcan B2 in 1961.* **Below** *'Who could ever forget their first glimpse of the huge white flying triangle?'* **Opposite page** *The shape of things to come—the Avro 707B prototype.*

Left *Boulton Paul P111, enthusi-astically flown in 1955 by Ben Gunn.*

Below left *A far cry from the Spitfire—the Supermarine 535 proto-type in 1950.*

Above right *Swift F4 and UFOs—in fact, Vulcans and Avro 707s in 1953.*

Right *Foretaste of variable sweep—the Short SB5 in 1953.*

Below *148 Squadron Valiants at readiness for a 'scramble' in 1960.*

Above *The Viscount in 1950.* **Below and opposite page** *Swing wing—the all-important Multi Role Combat Aircraft—the Tornado.*

Above left *The record-breaking Fairey Delta 2 WG774 which, on March 10 1956, piloted by Peter Twiss, became the first aircraft in the world to exceed 1,000 mph. The airframe was later remodelled to become the BAC 221.*

Left *The BAC 221 single seat research aircraft incorporated the variable angle nose section, to become popularly known as the 'droop snoot'. Developed from the world record-breaking Fairey Delta 2, it was displayed by Godfrey Auty, Chief Test Pilot of the Corporation's Bristol Division. The wing shape also clearly foreshadows Concorde and the little '221 must be one of the most beautiful of all post-war aeroplanes.*

Above *Treble One's 18 Hunters in immaculate formation.*

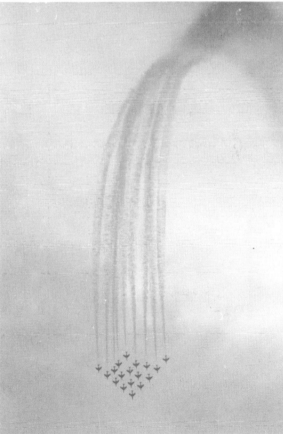

Right *Treble One 'pulling' at the recovery from their unforgettable low-level loop.*

Left *Avro-Canada CF-100 'Clunk' in 1955. Jan Zurakowski's 'Catherine Wheel' aerobatics, as earlier on the heavily loaded Meteor, are still recalled with awe by experts.*

Below left *The English Electric P1 in 1957.*

Below *The Folland Midge in 1954 —a beautiful and uncomplicated little fighter superbly displayed by Ted Tennant. Commercially it never 'took off' but its successor, the Gnat, was to be immortalised by the Red Arrows.*

Right *The Gloster Javelin made its Farnborough debut in 1952, a vintage year by any standards.*

Below right *The world's first hovercraft passengers aboard the SRN1 'flying cooling tower' in 1959.*

This page *The Fairey Rotodyne seen in 1961, flown to maximum advantage by Ron Gellatly.* **Above right** *The world's first operational jet bomber and one of the very few British aircraft to break the American sales barrier—the English Electric Canberra.* **Below right** *So clean and so effective—the Canberra T4 prototype.*

Above left *The DH 110 Sea Vixen prototype in 1952.* **Below left** *Sea Vixen FAW 1s in 1961.* **Above** *Vixen suckles Vixen, 1962.* **Below** *Ahead of its time? An FAW 2 in 1968.*

This page *The Lightning made a great impression at Farnborough flown by Roland Beamont, Desmond de Villiers, Peter Hillwood and Jimmy Dell, and when it stands on its tail with full reheat after a low pass it is still phenomenal.*

Opposite page *Sold to the Saudis —a Lightning piloted in 1966 by Jimmy Dell . . . and a Strikemaster in 1968.*

Left *Squeezing the moisture from a humid sky—a Phantom in a high speed run during 1968.*

Below left *Scrapped but not forgotten—the incomparable TSR2. Unfortunately, Farnborough crowds were never treated to this spectacle.*

Right *The Handley-Page 115 research delta with smoke generators to illustrate airflow during demonstration of low speed handling characteristics (1961).*

Right *The Bristol 188—an all-steel research airframe designed for supersonic skin temperature studies and powered by two enormous Gyron-Juniors (1962).*

Below *Fighting formation 92 Squadron Lightnings executed a demonstration 'scramble' in 1964—time 40 seconds from Very light to airborne.*

Close encounters

Every job has its 'perks'. That of the professional broadcaster is no exception. Frankly, the necessity to generate two major television programmes in the week of the Farnborough show can scarcely be described as an enjoyable experience. But there is one great consolation—the sheer thrill of actually flying from time to time in the Display. Thanks to their patience and co-operation, it has been my privilege over the years to fly with some of the greatest test pilots in the world. Without exception they have proved the kindest and most considerate of men. They belong to a very special brotherhood, and to be admitted to their ranks, however briefly and superficially, has been amongst the outstanding experiences of my life.

Broadcasting to the public from an aeroplane in flight presents considerable difficulties even in these days of advanced communication. Add the problem of matching television pictures to the commentary and you are in for headaches.

In the early years of the BBC's radio and television coverage of Farnborough, everything was done 'live'. Radio was first to enjoy the advantages of the tape recorder, and provided that the problems of 'background noise' could be overcome, the sky was no longer the limit. When the advent of video-tape began to revolutionise television, it became the practice at airshows to record the television rehearsal in case bad weather interfered with the intended 'live' coverage on the day of transmission. The next step was to record certain important items which could not be fitted into that section of the flying programme covered by the 'live' transmission. Finally, as the technique for editing video-tape on site became available to the Outside Broadcast Units, it was clear that the best way to give the viewing public the widest possible coverage was to abandon almost entirely the purists' concept of 'the live OB'. I choose deliberately the words 'almost entirely'. The limited time available to record and edit the video-tape with its accom-panying sound effects has meant that, as often as not, I have had to do my commentary 'live' as the recorded and edited pictures are transmitted. As will be appreciated this is a somewhat nerve-wracking task since the margin for error is precisely zero. It is much more difficult than doing a 'live' commentary to 'live' pictures, during which there is a dynamic relationship between the producer directing the cameras and his commentator, to whose words he is listening and, hopefully, responding.

On one such occasion—to be precise in 1972—my friend John Blake was 'sitting in' during my ordeal. His brilliant Public Address commentaries now enliven almost every air show in the country, including Farnborough. Although he never admitted it, I am sure that Dennis Monger, the BBC producer responsible—and also an old friend and colleague of many television adventures—had thoughtfully invited John to be present against the possibility of his ever having to replace me at the microphone, for whatever reason. From my point of view, John Blake within earshot was nothing but acceptable since however meticulous one's preparation a last minute question often arises in the pressure of the moment, and his knowledge is encyclopaedic. In the daunting task of preparation for air show commentaries I have been singularly blessed. Since 1970 I have enjoyed the unfailing assistance of a fellow enthusiast. His name is Andy Tallack; he is a Stage Manager with the BBC's Outside Broadcasts team, and he is the most willing and generous collaborator ever to walk miles in the rain to find the answer to a question. Fortunately our interests coincide. He too is a lover of aero-planes and motor-cars—preferably old ones. Himself an amateur pilot, he is totally unflappable, and a delightful companion as well as being super-lative at his job. We have shared many notable

Opposite page *Early television . . . and middle period radio.*

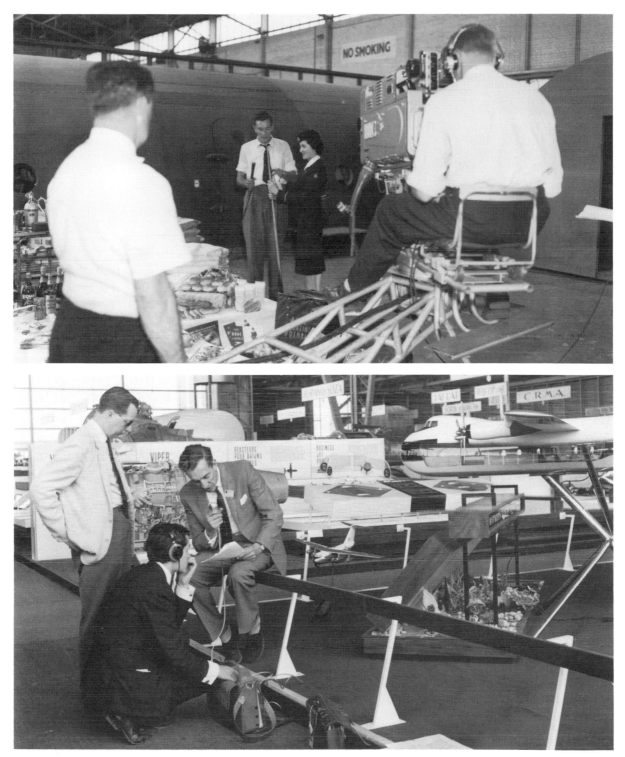

assignments, from the last home-coming of *Ark Royal* to the Festival of Remembrance, as well as Farnborough, and I believe every air show covered by the BBC since he joined its staff.

Concentration is fundamental to success in a broadcast of this kind and within minutes of starting that 1972 commentary I had completely forgotten my guest. But as I embarked upon the Harrier sequence, I noticed out of the corner of my eye that John Blake was very busy with his felt pen on a card identical to those on which I make my notes for each aircraft in the display. When he tentatively pushed the card towards me I snatched it with the sinking feeling that he may have spotted some error in what I had been saying. Not a bit of it. Beneath a delightful cartoon of the aircraft John had composed one of his instant limericks;

> 'A remarkable beast is the Harrier;
> It takes off very close to the barrier.
> It can lift enough stores
> To start several wars,
> From a wood or a beach or a carrier.'

I instantly read it aloud, of course, and had the satisfaction of watching John's jaw drop.

But to return to the problems of the airborne television commentary: Given the use of one of the aircraft's VHF channels it is clearly possible to record the speech transmission on the ground at the same time as the images of the TV cameras. A problem of synchronisation arises if the speech is recorded separately, either on the aircraft's on-board recorder, or a BBC machine suitably secured in the aeroplane—itself no small problem. As home-movie enthusiasts will appreciate the requirement is for a 'synch mark'. The conventional clapper board is, for obvious reasons, scarcely appropriate.

On one occasion, when we had asked Raynham Hanna to record his own commentary as he demonstrated Adrian Swire's Spitfire, it was agreed that his 'synch mark' would be a raised arm from the cockpit and the spoken word 'Now' immediately prior to take-off. Ray nearly broke his arm in the slipstream from the propeller.

A third method, only possible on aeroplanes of-fering sufficient space, is to embark a film cameraman and sound recordist and do the job the old fashioned way. This was the technique we employed when I opened our Farnborough '72 programme from the flight deck of Concorde.

I had known Brian Trubshaw since long before the Concorde project and his Deputy Chief Test Pilot, John Cochrane, had shared the commentary with me on our live coverage of Concorde 001's maiden flight by André Turcat at Toulouse on March 2 1969. A photograph, signed by Brian

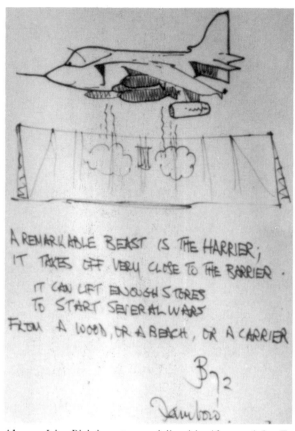

Above *John Blake's cartoon and limerick.* **Above right** *En route to Concorde's flight deck past electronic flight monitoring equipment which played a vital role in the prototype development programme.* **Right** *Concorde proving flight with 'Cap'n' Brian Trubshaw, Sir Douglas Bader and (left) Sir Harry Broadhurst.*

Trubshaw, John Cochrane and the whole crew of Concorde 002's first flight at Filton the following month, which we also covered 'live', adorns my study.

'Trubby' and John had both argued strongly in favour of this Farnborough exercise although it had not been received with universal acclaim amongst the 'Jacks in Office', mostly Ministry men, who seemed intent upon making life as difficult as possible for those two devoted and enthusiastic pilots.

Even as late as 1972 the future of Concorde was fraught with political hazard and its appearance at Farnborough had more than passing significance.

We flew in from Fairford—John Cochrane in command. The weather was marginal, and I shall never forget his total dedication to the task of making in four or five passes the maximum possible impression on the crowd. Everything was calculated in split second detail and John reefed the pride of British aviation around the sky—in his own words—'Just like demonstrating a big military aeroplane'. There was only one betrayal of the effort involved. Approaching the top of a steep climbing turn pulling better than 3G through low, broken cloud in visibility which could only be described as lousy, he suddenly muttered 'Christ! I've lost the runway.' It was somewhere behind his right shoulder at the time. But as we swooped down out of the turn he was bang on the centre-line: a trivial example perhaps but nevertheless typical of the skill, courage and determination exemplified by the unparalleled achievement of the entire Flight Development Programme of the world's first supersonic airliner.

I have never attempted to conceal that given the chance I prefer to publicise rather than criticise British achievement. In 1968 another such opportunity arose when that remarkable 'Man about Aviation' Sir Peter Masefield was Chairman of the Beagle Aircraft Co. In 1953 as Chief Executive of BEA he had managed to persuade the relevant authorities that it would be a good idea to enter a Viscount in, of all things, the New Zealand air-race from London to Christchurch. Since a primary objective was to generate maximum publicity for the world's first turbo-prop airliner, he had invited me to join the crew as acting unpaid Fourth Pilot and

The New Zealand air-race. Australians and New Zealanders turned out in their thousands to see the world's first prop-jet airliner.
Opposite page *'Droop snoots all'—BAC 221, Concorde and . . .*

broadcaster. The Viscount was beaten to Christchurch only by the Canberras of the RAF and RAAF. We got there in 40 hours and 43 minutes—considerably longer than today's scheduled 747 service. But it was a remarkable adventure by any standards, and no mean achievement for a medium-range prop-jet.

Consequently, when 15 years later Sir Peter decided to display the entire Beagle range at Farnborough in a single formation—aptly dubbed 'The Beagle Pack'—I was offered the ride, microphone in hand. My purpose was merely to record a piece for radio. The so-called EMI Midget Recorder—enormous by today's standards—was by then BBC regulation equipment for roving reporters, so there were no technical difficulties and a good time was had by all.

But the memory of that flight is sad for two reasons. With the notable exception of the Pup, which became the Bulldog, none of the Beagle aircraft proved a commercial success for the simple reason that they were never given the chance. With 18 of the 206 Series III sold into the United States, and no less than 150 orders placed for the 242 light twin, including one for Sir Jack Brabham—who was at that time setting the aviation trend to be followed by other leading men in motor racing like Colin Chapman and Graham Hill—the company ran out

of money. Denied the financial backing of Pressed Steel by motor industry politics, the Government in the person of Anthony Wedgwood Benn delivered the coup de grâce. Of £6 million then available from Government funds for immediate industrial aid he devoted the whole sum to the dying ship building industry of the Clyde instead of accepting expert advice to allocate up to £2 million of it to Beagle. It was Britain's last chance to win a share of the American light 'plane market.

On a more personal note, the sadness of the story centres on Peewee Judge with whom I flew on that occasion. I was to see him killed at Farnborough two years later when the rotors collapsed on the little Airmark WA.117 autogyro which he was demonstrating with typical verve and abandon. Had Beagle not been betrayed, 'Peewee' would not have joined Airmark and we should have been spared the loss of a man brave enough to overcome considerable physical deformity to become a test pilot.

Ever since the days of Icarus it would seem, aviation has been as fraught with tragedy and disappointment as it is rich in triumph and reward. Very early in my association with Farnborough, in 1953, I flew in a de Havilland Comet with John Cunningham. Less than a year later, three of the first 22 Mk I Comets had broken up in mid-air. These early metal fatigue tragedies struck the

Above and opposite page *'Gear up and travelling'—but not off the ski-jump: the Hawk shows its paces.* Below *One of the 'perks'—flying the Redifon DC10 simulator for the 1976 Farnborough TV programme.*

world's first jet airliner a crippling blow which effectively destroyed its brilliant commercial promise, and set in train the unprecedented research programme at Farnborough itself, from which not least to benefit was the Boeing Corporation whose 707s soon scooped the pool of the world market.

Later in 1962, when he first displayed the Trident, I flew with John Cunningham again. Explaining the triplication of all the flight systems as well as the engine configuration he suggested this to be the derivation of the name, a fact no doubt lost upon the millions who have subsequently profited from the aircraft's pioneer hands-off landing capability, in the development of which John Cunningham of course played a key rôle. It is certainly not for me to comment on the way John Cunningham handles an aeroplane. I have heard many leading test pilots credit him with the best displays of big civil aeroplanes ever seen at Farnborough, and certainly his contribution to British aviation during his 42 years of active flying to date must be hard to equal.

Curiously enough I may be able to claim the questionable distinction of having drawn another very distinguished test pilot once again into the Farnborough Display on the eve of his retirement, when in his own words, he 'really had decided not to perform again'.

Duncan Simpson is one of those amazing men who seem untouched by the passing years. His last great professional achievement was his leading rôle in the Flight Development of the Hawker Siddeley Hawk. He displayed it at Farnborough in 1974 within days of his maiden flight in the proto-type. In fact the trip to Farnborough was only the Hawk's ninth flight. At the end of the show it had completed 25 sorties and never missed a day—an almost unbelievable achievement for a brand new aeroplane. Interviewing him at that time, both on the television screen and off it, he looked the debonair young man who is every girl's dream of a test pilot. In fact he started flying with the RAF in 1948 and had been in every Farnborough display since '56, having joined Hawker two years earlier after a tour with the Air Fighting Development Unit. Just before the next show in 1976, two years after its debut, I rather cheekily asked Hawker Siddeley if I could ride in the Hawk. Since it was intended to put the aeroplane through its paces with the dash demanded by its performance, the test pilot originally allocated the task apparently, and not unreasonably, expressed no uncertain reservations, viz. 'Not bloody likely', or words to that effect. It was at this point that Duncan moved in. He was, af-

ter all, Chief Test Pilot and whether or not I flew in the Hawk was therefore ultimately his responsibility. Being the gentleman he is, he tactfully suggested 'A little fly around, Raymond; so that you can get the feel of the thing, and I'll chat you through as we go along.' I realised, of course, that his primary objective was to determine whether I was still capable of coherent speech during high speed low level aerobatics. We took off immediately after the Press Preview and after a tentative wingover or two, and a few minutes following those beloved words 'You have control', we re-entered the Farnborough circuit with permission to perform the Display routine. It was every bit as stimulating and impressive as I had known it would be. The aircraft clearly had all the character of its thoroughbred lineage. After landing Duncan said casually 'You'll find I may tighten it up a bit when we do it for real, Raymond. You know how it is in the heat of the moment. But I don't expect we'll be pulling very much more G.' I had noticed 5 + on the meter already.

In fact when, on the following day, we did it for real we pulled well over 6G + and had it not been for Duncan's meticulous briefing and gentle introduction, I am sure my commentary would never have caught up with the action—let alone

been the one-jump ahead necessary for television. I knew that from my point of view the key moment was the quick roll and Derry turn off the top of a steep straight inverted climb from a low pass. I wanted to make the point of the amazing inverted view of Farnborough through the beautiful canopy, of the Hawk, but our dummy run had proved there wasn't time during that sequence. I explained my problem, and Duncan immediately suggested, and duly executed, an additional inverted fly past up the whole length of the runway.

The Hawk's 'slot' in the display was 4½ minutes. Douglas Hespe, who has been responsible for editing our Farnborough programme for many years, is a personal friend. But I know that he would not have included the entire sequence in our main transmission had he not considered it worthwhile television.

But with every respect and gratitude to Duncan Simpson and all the other pilots who have been kind enough to put up with me and my microphone aboard—not excluding the epic outing I shared with Peter Twiss in a Gannet for the Coronation Review of the Fleet Air Arm in 1953—I owe my most unforgettable sorties as an airborne commentator to John Farley and the famous two-seat Harrier G-VTOL.   □

Below left *Test pilot John Cochrane shares the TV commentary on Concorde's first flight at Toulouse (an 'off-screen' picture).* **Above** *Trident debut in 1962—up to 103 passengers and the world's first airliner with built-in automatic landing capability. De Havilland displayed three Tridents in BEA livery during the show.* **Below** *However, the first aircraft in the world to be fitted with an automatic landing system was the Vickers Valetta as displayed by Smiths Aviation, the Ministry of Aviation and the College of Aeronautics, Cranfield, in 1962.* **Overleaf** *Cartoon reproduced from the September 6 1957 issue of* The Aeroplane *by courtesy of the artist.*

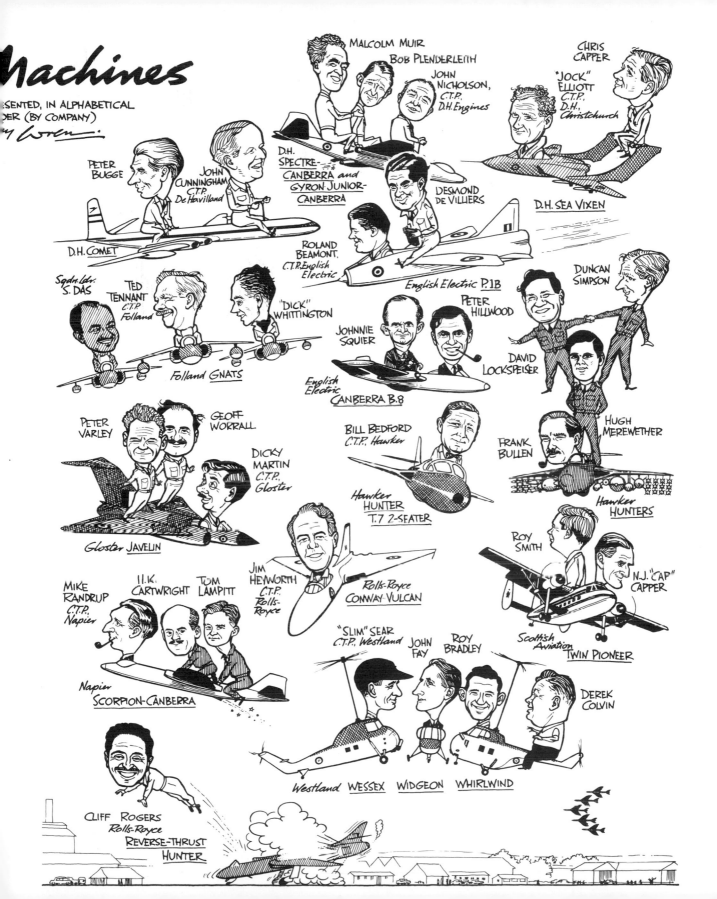

Machines

PRESENTED, IN ALPHABETICAL ORDER (BY COMPANY)

MALCOLM MUIR
BOB PLENDERLEITH
JOHN NICHOLSON, C.T.P. D.H. Engines
CHRIS CAPPER
"JOCK" ELLIOTT C.T.P. D.H., Christchurch

PETER BUGGE
JOHN CUNNINGHAM C.T.P. De Havilland
D.H. SPECTRE-CANBERRA and GYRON-JUNIOR-CANBERRA
DESMOND DE VILLIERS
D.H. SEA VIXEN

D.H. COMET

ROLAND BEAMONT. C.T.P. English Electric
English Electric P.1B
DUNCAN SIMPSON
PETER HILLWOOD

Sqdn. Ldr. S. DAS
TED TENNANT C.T.P. Folland
"DICK" WHITTINGTON
Folland GNATS

JOHNNIE SQUIER
English Electric CANBERRA B.8

DAVID LOCKSPEISER
HUGH MEREWETHER

PETER VARLEY
GEOFF WORRALL
DICKY MARTIN C.T.P., Gloster

BILL BEDFORD C.T.P. Hawker
FRANK BULLEN

Gloster JAVELIN

Hawker HUNTER T.7 2-SEATER
Hawker HUNTERS

ROY SMITH
N.J. "CAP" CAPPER

MIKE RANDRUP C.T.P., Napier
H.K. CARTWRIGHT
TOM LAMPITT
JIM HEYWORTH C.T.P. Rolls-Royce
Rolls-Royce CONWAY-VULCAN

Scottish Aviation TWIN PIONEER

Napier SCORPION-CANBERRA

"SLIM" SEAR C.T.P. Westland
JOHN FAY
ROY BRADLEY
DEREK COLVIN

Westland WESSEX WIDGEON WHIRLWIND

CLIFF ROGERS Rolls-Royce REVERSE-THRUST HUNTER

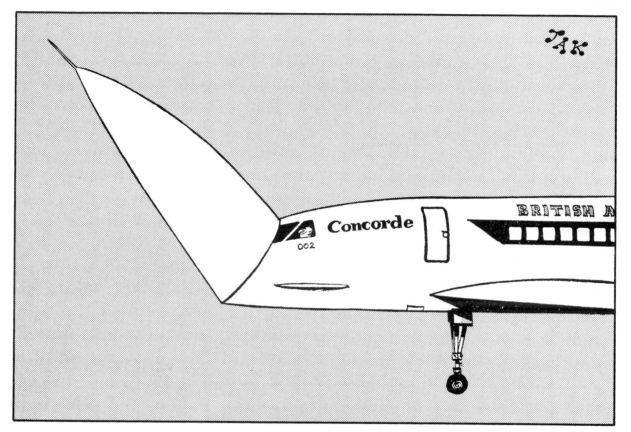

Above *The cartoonist's salute to the Filton-assembled Concorde prototype 002 and its chief test pilot, Brian Trubshaw! The JAK caption read ' "Tower to Trubshaw, tower to Trubshaw, stop showing off!" '*

Left *A Gannet in 1951. For me the Coronation Review of the Fleet Air Arm in 1953 with Peter Twiss at 'the sharp end' and Slim Lear on the starboard wing—sometimes. The Gannet helped blaze the trail of Britain's leadership in 'prop-jets', sadly relinquished to the US.*

Above right *Colleague Ken Pragnell (BBC Radio) caught off guard on the Armstrong-Whitworth Gloster stand at Le Bourget when the Argosy was still a model.*

Right *Armstrong-Whitworth Argosy at Farnborough in 1959.*

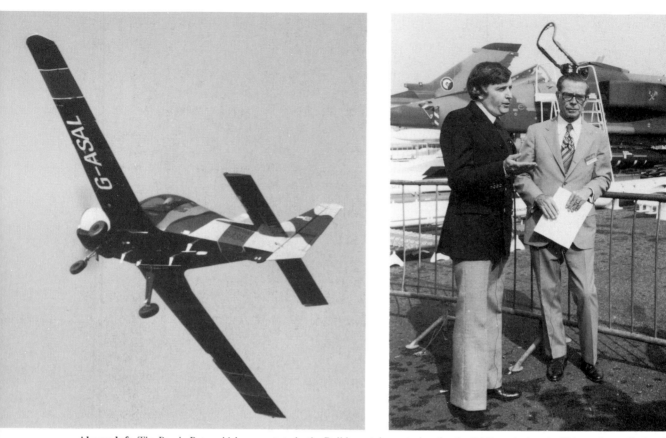

Above left *The Beagle Pup, which grew up to be the Bulldog—primary trainer for the RAF, replacing the Chipmunk, as displayed in 1978.* **Above right** *Like father, like son: Robert Gardner of British Aerospace with Warren Kramer of McDonnell Douglas.* **Below** *Scottish Aviation Bullfinch, four-seater progeny of the Bulldog, née Pup.*

Above *The Beagle B 206, described as a 'superbly equipped five-seat air-limousine'. With two 260 hp Rolls Royce Continentals it was aimed at the US market—but was nipped in the bud by lack of finance, government or private.* Below *The Beagle in 1964—Britain's last chance to penetrate the US light aircraft market.*

Above *Another member of the Beagle pack—the Airedale in 1961.* **Below** *The amazing little Wallis Airmark autogyro.*

Straight up

The development of jet VTOL is one of the great sagas of British aviation. Adequately to chronicle it even as seen at Farnborough alone must be done elsewhere.

The story started with the Rolls Royce experiments with their Flying Bedstead in 1953. The company firmly nailed its colours to the mast of multiple engines and designed the RB108 turbo-jet specifically to meet the requirement. It was heralded as the first of a new generation of vertical lift engines, and airframes were commissioned to prove the point. Short's SC1 made its Farnborough appearance in 1959 and Tom Brooke-Smith lifted it briefly off the ground. Safely down again his sigh of relief was almost audible. The following year was more impressive. The SC1's four RB108 lift engines achieved VTO and Brooke-Smith proved his mastery of the complex control system by inducing transition to conventional flight with the aid of the fifth '108. He then did a couple of conventional circuits at around 250 mph, and landed vertically.

But there were those who questioned the viability of a five-engined single-seater even for experimental purposes. Amongst them was Sir Sydney Camm's Hawker team headed by future projects engineer Ralph Hooper.

Already their single Bristol Pegasus engined vectored thrust prototype P1127 was achieving tethered hovers in secret tests. Bill Bedford recalls that having had his leg broken in a car accident in Germany he achieved a unique distinction. He bullied the doctors into certifying him 'Fit civil test pilot—tethered hovering only.'

With typical Hawker showmanship the P1127 stole the Farnborough show in 1962. Bill Bedford and Hugh Merewether did very short rolling take-offs in their '1127s as David Lockspeiser flashed in on a Hunter 66. The three aircraft then executed a typical high performance fighter display, the '1127s landed vertically, and the Hunter flew off as if nothing had happened. The Short SC1 was consigned to pure research at the Aerodynamics Flight, RAE Bedford, and never appeared in public again. But ironically the full technical information gained from its lift engines, together with the wing aerodynamics of the Fairey Delta 2, were handed in a misplaced gesture of co-operation to the French, who instantly applied the fruits of this pioneering

Right *Ralph Hooper. In 1957 he was Future Projects Engineer Chief Designer for the P1127 Kestrel. It is arguable that, without him, the Harrier would never have happened.*

research to their own VTOL ambitions. But the way ahead for the Hawker team was far from clear.

In 1964 three P1127s, now named the 'Kestrel', again executed a brilliant Farnborough display at just subsonic speeds.

Meantime there had been a major controversy within NATO concerning the supersonic version of the '1127 which the Hawker team had on their drawing board as the P1154. The row also involved the conflicting requirements of the RN and the RAF in which both refused to compromise. There was also a French contender called the Balzac which had sprung from a cross between the SC1 and the Mirage and had no less than eight Rolls Royce RB162 lift engines. It is significant that Hawker still planned a single Bristol Pegasus engine, now developed by Sir Stanley Hooker to provide 750 + mph at tree top height, and the government imposed merger between Rolls Royce and the Bristol engine division had yet to come. The bitter arguments were abruptly terminated by the newly elected Labour Government in 1963 when Denis Healey cancelled outright the P1154—as well as the TSR2.

The tripartite Kestrel Evaluation Squadron which had been set up with pilots from Britain, Germany and the United States at the end of 1964 was disbanded after nine months, having completed a far-ranging sequence of trials. Despite the glowing reports filed to their own governments by the German and American pilots, only the US took action. The German aircraft from the Tripartite Squadron were acquired in addition to their own and successful multi-service V/STOL trials were carried out in the USA. The aircraft were then divided for V/STOL evaluation and research at Edwardes Air Force Base and at NASA Langley, Virginia. Although the Germans sent observers to the initial US multi-service trials, their Kestrel pilots were given strict instructions by their hierarchy that regardless of their enthusiasm for the Kestrel and V/STOL, they were to 'shut up' on the subject within the GAF and Ministry of Defence

since V/STOL was not a way the German air force intended to go. In the States, however, although not involved in the Kestrel trials, the US Marines saw the light and after a thorough evaluation they ordered the Harrier unilaterally in 1967.

But the Squadron's work was invaluable to the RAF in formulating its own Operational Requirement for the P1127. Not until 1967 was it named the 'Harrier', and even years after it had won its RAF wings in every way there were those in Whitehall, and indeed the Service itself, who appeared curiously reluctant to seize and exploit its maximum potential. None were Harrier pilots. Not until it had lost its argument to retain at least one capital ship did the Royal Navy make up its mind to accept the Harrier. The specially developed maritime version, the 'Sea Harrier', still powered by a single vectored Pegasus, made its long awaited Farnborough debut in 1978. Bill Bedford had performed the first deck landings, take-offs and operational trials with a P1127 aboard HMS *Ark Royal* 15 years before.

To this day the future of Britain's undisputed world lead in jet VTOL remains in jeopardy. Further development has been effectively relinquished to McDonnell Douglas under a complex licensing deal, and it is no secret that even this has not been received with universal acclaim in the US.

If the brilliant design, development and flying of two decades is not to be lost to this country, courageous decisions must be taken now. Supersonic VTOL is well within the capability of the successors to the original Hawker team from whose grasp it was stupidly snatched in 1963. It is too much to hope that a more enlightened Government may profit from the mistakes of its predecessors, authorise and finance the necessary engine development by Rolls Royce, commission an operational research vehicle, and exploit to the full the sales potential of an aircraft as eminently desirable to the friendly air forces of the world as was the Hunter, and its 'thin-wing' supersonic successor could have been? □

Above right *The P1127 in 1962. From their first appearance, the Hawker Siddeley jet VTOL team have invariably stolen the show.*
Right *Rolls Royce Flying Bedstead—properly known as an 'engine thrust measuring rig'.*

Left *USMC Harrier at Farnborough in 1970.*

Short SC1 seen in 1960 **(below)** *and 1961* **(left)***. With five Rolls Royce engines its jet VTOL performance was no match for the Kestrel's single Pegasus.*

Opposite page *Land and sea— 'laser nose' RAF Harrier and the RN's Sea Harrier.*

Something else

I first flew with John Farley in the famous two-seat Harrier G-VTOL in 1974. *Aeroplane Monthly* was kind enough to ask me to report my 1974 impressions and I titled the article 'Something Else'. I can still think of no better summary, and I believe everyone fortunate enough to have experienced at first hand the unbelievable performance of the Harrier would agree.

John Farley is the quiet, unassuming archetypal modern test pilot who has retained the boyish enthusiasm and zest for flying of yesteryear. His mastery of his profession is total. He is the essence of courtesy and patience but he does not tolerate fools gladly. Like many of his kind he is blessed with a dry sense of humour, which can be devastating.

In fact, the technique for controlling the world's first operational vectored thrust aircraft, and indeed the control system itself, was devised and developed from scratch by Ralph Hooper and his Hawker Siddeley design team. In the embryonic days experimental test pilots Bill Bedford and Hugh Merewether pioneered the dangerous and daunting task of evolving the V/STOL and hovering techniques. Other pilots took part in the programme: in the words of Bill Bedford—'None more avidly or professionally than the company's now Chief Test Pilot, John Farley'.

From the outset Sir Sydney Camm and his team had insisted that, despite powerful argument to the contrary from Rolls Royce, it was a misconception to employ separate engines for lift and thrust. Hence, instead of the conventional jet pipe, the swivelling nozzles for the Pegasus engine were evolved. This ensured simplicity and offered the total installed thrust for conventional flight. However, it was essential for the pilot to have full control at air speeds much lower than those at which the normal flying controls became effective and therefore some additional forces had to be put at his disposal. For this purpose small 'puffer jets' are installed at the extremities of the air frame, known in the trade as jet reaction controls. Their energy is derived by bleeding off a small percentage of the main thrust. It was the unanimous opinion of the designers and pilots from the outset that the operation of these puffers should be automatically actuated by the movement of the stick and rudder in the cockpit.

Thus, if operating below the stalling speed the pilot wishes to lift his port wing he simply moves the control column to the right as would be his instinctive response. High pressure air is then expelled from the port puffer and the reaction raises the wing. The greater the stick movement the greater the rate of roll. Similarly, fore and aft movement of the control column will raise or lower the nose, and left or right rudder pedal will cause the aircraft to yaw to the left or right respectively. In effect this means that the aircraft attitude is controlled on the stick, the heading on the rudder and the height with the normal pilot's throttle when the aircraft is at the hover. The bleed air feeding the puffers cuts off automatically as the nozzle selector lever is moved forward through the last 20° of its arc. Although the test pilots resisted cockpit complexity, there was, of course, one inescapable addition—the nozzle selector lever controlling the direction of the thrust vector. It is mounted in a quadrant beside the throttle, and works in the same direction as the anticipated response, ie, push it forward and you go faster—thrust vector aft; pull it back and you go slower—thrust vector pointing downwards.

Two factors must be borne in mind. Actuation of the puffers reduces the total thrust available to support the aircraft. Secondly, inclination of the fuselage inescapably governs the direction of the main thrust which is only aimed fore and aft by the nozzle selector lever. Effectively this interreaction between attitude of the airframe and direction of the lift generated by the vectored thrust is the key to the Harrier's outstanding capabilities. It has also been

the cause of more than one disastrous mistake, even
by pilots of vast conventional experience. It is as if
the aircraft is balanced on the tip of a pencil
attached to a hinge in line with its wing and capable
of opening 98° from the pencil pointing towards the
tail. Try fiddling about with a pencil between your
fingers and it will soon be apparent that the range of
attitude and recovery, though astonishing, is clearly
finite.

After we had been quietly chatting by G-VTOL
for about 45 minutes I realised I had been given
the most detailed, articulate and totally comprehensible pre-flight briefing it had ever been my good
fortune to enjoy. It was the definitive lecture on the
theory and practice of Harrier flying. Farley had
cautiously accepted the proposal, initiated by Bill
Bedford, his predecessor as Chief Test Pilot of
Hawker Siddeley's Harrier Division, that I should
take a ride in G-VTOL during the Display. Like his
colleague Duncan Simpson, he quietly suggested a
short familiarisation course around Dunsfold as an
opening gambit. Almost within seconds of a short
rolling take-off he invited me to fly the aeroplane.
Minutes later: 'Why don't you try a roll
Raymond?'

'What, now?', We were at about 1,000 feet and
300 knots crossing Dunsfold airfield at the time. So
I did, and as Farley knew perfectly well my confidence in both him and the Harrier was from that
moment absolute.

After stabilising the Harrier in a hover at about
30 feet, he put his hands high and told me to move
the aircraft very slowly and gently forward, back-
ward, sideways, and to turn in the manner he had
explained before we took off. What is more I could
do it—and did. A total contrast to my brief and
twitchy attempts to perform exactly the same
manoeuvres on previous occasions in conventional
helicopters.

Even so, without the total confidence born of that
brief but brilliantly contrived introduction to
Harrier flying, I would almost certainly have
screamed a few minutes later. Back at Farnborough
and landed on the pad, John executed his opening
display gambit—the Farley Special take off. He
would never describe it as such himself, but I
believe that neither his test pilot colleagues nor RAF
Harrier Squadron pilots would quarrel with the
definition. It consists of a vertical lift off just high
enough to clear the tail of the ground. He then pulls
the nose instantly up to an angle approaching 60°.
From this alarming attitude, with zero airspeed, the
aeroplane claws its way into the sky—agonisingly
slowly at first, but in seconds shooting up like a
rocket. It is essentially a display manoeuvre, and

*'The most detailed and totally comprehensible pre-flight briefing'
from John Farley.*

surely one of the most spectacular ever devised.

Of the Harrier, John Farley says 'It is not a difficult aeroplane to fly. But it is also an aeroplane on which it is very easy to kill yourself—if you ignore the rules about how it works.'

John Farley's skill as a Harrier display pilot results from his highly developed juggling with the 'pencil' of thrust on which he balances his aircraft, without ever ignoring for a milli-second where the pencil is pointing in relation to the ground.

In order to accentuate this unique characteristic of the Harrier for the benefit of the Farnborough crowd in the '76 Display, Farley borrowed the Red Arrows' trick of injecting paraffin at will into his jet stream. The resultant column of smoke clearly demonstrated the angle selected for the vectored thrust. Seen from the right angle, and Farley was at pains to ensure that all sections of the enclosures were treated to the appropriate side elevation whenever he 'made smoke', it was a brilliantly successful ploy from the point of view—in every sense—of the paying public.

But it is not only the public who watch the Farnborough Display. The governing authority who decides what is or is not acceptable is the SBAC flying control committee chaired by the Commanding Officer Experimental Flying Department Royal Aircraft Establishment Farnborough. The committee, a sort of college of cardinals, consists of some of the most respected British test pilots, both retired and active.

Treated to this first glimpse of John Farley's spectacular smoke signals at the Press Preview, Roland Beamont, amongst whose great achievements was the development of the Lightning, turned to his Display Committee colleague John Cunningham and enquired drily, 'What the devil does John think he's up to? He looks like the bloody Flying Scotsman—inverted.'

A further complication when exploring to its limits the Harrier's envelope of performance at low level is the insidious potential effect of sideslip. Until the Harrier has achieved about 100 knots, when the fin starts to become effective, the aircraft is short of natural directional stability. If sideslip develops it can be associated with a strong tendency to roll. Immediately in his eyeline on the nose of the Harrier is a simple wind vane designed to tell the pilot if sideslip is present. Additional anti-sideslip devices on the Harrier include yaw autostabilisation and rudder pedal shakers. Without it, more than one of his sensational display sequences would transgress even Farley's precisely determined frontiers of 'the acceptable risk factor'.

In my briefing John Farley said 'There are just one or two moments in the display, Raymond, when we're not too well placed should the fire go out. Of course it won't, but if it does, I promise I won't say a word. Not because I've gone off you or anything. It's just that there wouldn't be time. So if you see me go, you go. OK?' And then he added 'Most of the show, we've got all the time in the world.'

To my great delight I had to fly with John four times during the '74 show after our dummy run. The first time the quality of the BBC audio tape of my commentary recorded off the aircraft's VHF transmission was unacceptable. Second time around, we used the Harrier's on-board voice recorder—to John's great satisfaction. Then the cameras went on the blink, and I got the excuse for yet another ride.

In this display John Farley introduced me to two completely new flying experiences—in addition to that take-off, and of course the Harrier's hover and STOL capabilitites.

One was 'viffing', the unbelievable effect of using the vectored thrust to 'decelerate' the aeroplane from any speed up to maximum, and at the same time drive it into a turn so tight, and ever tightening, as to present a totally new concept in fighter pilot tactics. Full power is used; the din is terrific, and the whole aircraft batters and vibrates alarmingly, while at the same time the deceleration forces one forward as well as downwards in the harness—a totally unfamiliar feeling in a tight turn. At better than $6\frac{1}{2}$ G my tinted visor snapped down on my 'bone dome' and I thought for a panic-stricken moment that I was experiencing a startling new variety of 'blackout', or even more alarming, had been suddenly struck partially blind.

The other unforgettable moment came immediately after this shattering assault upon my ability to think straight, let alone talk.

Having reefed the Harrier round in the 'viff' to a stationary hover at 1,300 feet over the perimeter of the airfield, opposite and facing the crowd, John went into what he apologetically described as 'The Tu 144—with recovery'. This consists of sharply pointing the Harrier straight at the ground and thereafter using the vectored thrust to control the rate of descent in what appears an impossibly steep angle of approach to the landing pad. The procedure is, in fact, the reverse of that hair-raising take-off.

In those $4\frac{1}{2}$ minutes of John Farley's display we took off and landed twice: our flying speed ranged from zero to in excess of 500 knots three times: our altitude from about 50 feet at high speed to stationary at 1,000; he performed two wing overs, two quick

rolls, a Derry turn and an inverted fly-past; we
'viffed' and in the initial take off and first landing the
crowd watched an aeroplane in attitudes they had
never seen before. For me it was not what could be
honestly described as a comfortable ride. I have
never been 'banged about' so much in any aeroplane,
simply because no other aeroplane has the Harrier's
breathtaking ability to stop and go. It was the most
exciting flying imaginable. It was unforgettable, not
least because I was allowed the privilege of sharing
for those brief moments the experience of a world
master in the practice of his chosen craft.

Four years later in Farnborough 1978 came the
Harrier ski-jump, and again John Farley was kind
enough to give me a first-hand view in G-VTOL.
He had been primarily responsible for the development of this amazing technique over many
exhausting hours of the most exacting experimental
flying by day and night. The ski-jump, by literally
launching the aeroplane into the air at less than
flying speed, adds new dimensions to the Harrier's
operational capability. It is of fundamental importance to the Sea Harrier which made its debut at the
same show, but it also has enormous tactical potential for the RAF's Harrier force, and indeed that of
the US Marine Corps.

Seen from the cockpit it is again, quite simply,
'Something Else'. As before our previous excur-
sions John had quietly treated me to his impeccable
briefing, as well as arranging a couple of dummy-
runs 'to get the feel'.

'All aboard'.

Even though I therefore knew exactly what to expect and had seen his display at the Press Preview,
as we taxied to the take-off position, the ramp grew
higher and higher, and at the same time more and
more narrow. With G-VTOL stationary on the pad
at its foot, the whole exercise appeared quite impossible, and I was grateful for my previous experience of both the pilot and his aircraft.

I now know how it would feel if, by some Alice in
Wonderland magic, one were able to ride a paper
dart launched into the air by an energetic small boy.
Having been catapulted off an aircraft carrier I can
assert that it is an experience not in the same league.
The catapult simply hurls the aircraft and its
occupants down the deck and at flying speed they
become airborne. Not so off the ski-jump. Yet in
fact the actual flying technique during the Harrier
ski-jump is not nearly as complex, or 'dodgy' as
might be supposed.

Held on the brakes, the engine is run up to power
with the vectored thrust all the way aft. Brakes off,
the Harrier charges up the ramp to clear the end at
about 50 knots, with a nose-up attitude of whatever

the ramp angle—in the case of the Farnborough ramp 15°.

As the ramp is cleared, the pilot snaps the vector control to the 50° position and, supported by its thrust, the aircraft smoothly and very quickly accelerates until at about 150 knots and supported by its wings, the pilot completes the transition by returning his vector control to maximum forward thrust. Thanks to the Harrier's dynamic or 'thrust-bleed' control system, stability is maintained throughout by conventional use of rudder pedals and 'stick'.

The difficulty from my point of view was to explain what was going on during the take-off in the time available—3½ seconds from 'brakes off' to clear of the ramp.

As following my previous Farnborough flight with John Farley, and my Hawk ride with Duncan Simpson, I am very happy to report that my colleagues Dennis Monger and Douglas Hespe considered the whole sequence worthy of inclusion in the television transmission, with only one 'edit' of a few seconds when we disappeared in low cloud in our first steep wing-over after take off.

I still have the tapes from G-VTOL's on-board voice recorder. If Roy Plomley ever asks me to play 'Desert Island Discs' again I shall certainly include them in my limited luggage. The following is a transcript from the first of the 1978 recordings. The sequence starts with John Farley in the front cockpit as we start taxiing out towards my introduction to the art of ski-jumping by Harrier. The rising and falling whine of the Pegasus provides background music interspersed with occasional percussive intrusions from harshly distorted RT between Farnborough Tower and aircraft in the circuit at the end of the Wednesday display. Our breathing is audible via the oxygen mask microphones.

John Farley We'll just have to put up with it. [RT break-in]. After all, the object of the exercise tonight is for you just to get the feel of it. We'll try to make a recording over the top of it all, just to see what it's like. But you know how difficult it is to talk sensibly over someone else's conversation, don't you?
Raymond Baxter Yes, it's called television.
JF [chuckles] I know what you mean . . . Well you get a good view of the jump there.
RB Yeah. It's getting bigger and bigger.
JF [laughs] I like it . . . Standing on the right over there in that group of people by the ramp we have got John Fozzard, the erstwhile Chief Designer of the aeroplane—now a salesman.
RB Yeah?
JF And in front of us we've got Dick Ball who is

going to marshal us to the correct run-distance because . . . ooops! I see. OK, round again. [Farley turns the Harrier in its own length on the pad.] I wasn't watching him. I was watching the Dash 78 out of the corner of me eye . . . He's going to marshal us to the correct run-distance because it is by setting the run-distance that you set your end speed—the speed at which we'll get airborne of course.
RB I see.
JF We have no control over the speed we get airborne at, do we, other than the distance we allow ourselves to accelerate on the ground?
RB Right.
JF Do you understand?
RB Yes.
JF So he has to put us at the right place . . . Well he don't give me the slowdown signal, you see; he just gives me the gone too far signal which is . . .' [Laugh—pause as Farley turns the Harrier a second time. RT break in.]
RB It's that critical?
JF Well, only if we want to play the game for real, you know, and get it in the right place.
RB Yes, yes.
JF Right [in the swift monotone of pre-flight checks]. The voice recorder is on and running. Full flap is down. The throttle stop is at 97. I haven't done any accel checks—so we'll just do a couple of them [RT break in]. Engine accel checks are OK. STO stop going into 35° . . . and checking . . . showing 31 . . . that's OK. Trim going to 5½ . . . Setting the altimeter to nought. That's lovely. My pins are out. I took your pins out. The water I'm not using . . . [sing song]. We're ready for take-off . . . I'll just talk to Air Traffic and see what they've got to say . . . Tower—Harrier for take-off?
Farnborough Tower Roger. Is this the same as the last sortie?
JF A-firmative—to reland zero seven, sir.
Farnborough Tower [typical swift, slightly distorted RT] Roger. You want to watch for the chopper at low level on your right. When you have him in sight you are clear to take off; the wind light and variable.
JF Roger Harrier . . . OK, Raymond. I'm going up to 55 per cent rpm on the brakes which is all we can hold at that stage . . . Now I'm engaging the nose-wheel steering ready to keep straight up the ramp . . . Brakes off and full throttle . . . And 'way we go [talking fast] and as we run up the ramp . . .
RB Jesus!
JF [talking continuously and very fast] I've got me hand on the nozzle lever and as we get to the end [the Harrier shoots off the ramp] bingo, we put the nozzles down, and it's coasting its way through the

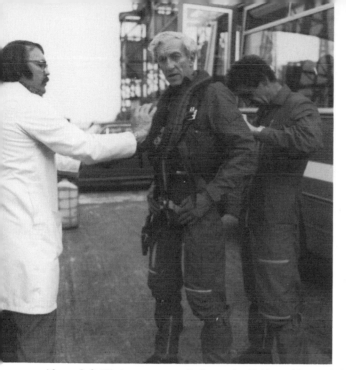

Above left *Kitting out—as meticulous as in all things.* **Above right** *Making the point.* **Below** *'Jesus!'*

Raymond,
Thank you so much for coming along (and for not telling everybody that British Aerospace pilots do it with their eyes shut)
Yours
John

Opposite page *Flight certification—John Farley's signature.* **Above** *Into the air like a paper dart Sea Harrier off the ski jump in 1978. Next step—supersonic VTOL: yet another world 'first' which Britain will let slip to her cost.*

sky, slowly building up speed. We're going now from 55, we've increased to 105. There the thing will fly away—so I'm pushing the nozzle lever slowly forward now and as we get to 150 knots we're fully flying on the wing. [1 second pause.] Well, there we are. There was no great pain to that, was there?

RB That's amazing. It still took me by surprise.

JF Did it, yea?

RB Yea. I agree no great pain but the jump off the top of the ski jump is just unbelievable.

JF [laughs]

RB You know, you'd never think it possible would you?

JF OK. Well, let's put the jet back on the ground and try it again, and this time you follow me through on the controls. OK?

RB Not 'arf!

That, I repeat, was a recording of the first rehearsal. When we 'did it for real', the combination of recorded commentary and pictures from the ground television cameras continued throughout John Farley's 3½-minute demon-

stration: from the ski-jump take-off and steep climbing turn right to 1,500 feet; steep wing-over left and dive to the Display Line; low-level pass up the runway (50 feet, nearly 500 knots); steep pull up and two quick rolls; 'viff' left; Tu 144 with recovery; vertical landing on pad.

When I was a little boy, I learned to play a violin, rather badly. When I was little more than a boy I learned to fly an aeroplane, somewhat better. But I know enough about both to appreciate mastery when I meet it. In both, co-ordination, touch and timing, as well as creative flair, hard work, sensitivity and self-discipline are amongst the pre-requisites of greatness. It is the experience born of years which leads me to suggest, in all humility, that display pilots of the calibre of a handful of names in any generation are the equals in every way of those, similarly few, whose medium is a musical instrument. It is called virtuosity. But there is one significant difference. If the master violinist is a milli-second off an inflection or a single cycle off the pitch of a note, only he may notice. If the master display pilot makes a comparable error, he may well be dead.   □

Big beasties

It is sad that two of the largest aircraft ever seen at Farnborough were white elephants from the drawing board. I count myself lucky to have seen both fly since neither was airborne sufficiently to have been seen by many. They were the Bristol Brabazon and the Saunders-Roe Princess.

Doubly sad is that one of the great names in British aviation, Lord Brabazon of Tara, should be linked with the first of a disastrous series of post-war Government blunders. But the story is not entirely without merit. As early as 1942, when the war was far from won, a Government committee sanctioned by Churchill and chaired by Brabazon considered how best to insure Britain's post-war civil aviation against the threat of American policy. The US aircraft industry, despite its magnificent war effort, never lost sight of the potential of the long range civil airliner. Without the Douglas DC-3 Dakota the Royal Air Force could not have met its wartime transport commitments. Indeed they would not have been planned. Britain had not produced the equivalent of the Dakota and by 1942 its American successors were well past the drawing board.

The Brabazon Committee drew up proposals for five or more aircraft to cover the range. The biggest was the Brabazon. Surprisingly it was the first to be commissioned, and work actually started at Filton in 1943. The Mk I prototype took no less than 6½ years to complete, by which time it was obsolete. But it was the world's biggest aeroplane. It had the same span as the American Convair B-36—230 feet—but a longer fuselage. It had a 'dry' weight of 145,000 lb (70 tons) and a designed operating weight of up to 300,000 lb. It was the world's first aircraft to have power-operated controls (with no manual over-ride) and to employ electrically operated engine controls. It had eight 2,500 hp Bristol Centaurus radials, coupled to drive four sets

Below *Two rare pictures of Brabazon G-AGPW at the 1950 Display.* **Opposite page** *The following year the queues to visit the Brabazon were as long as they were for Concorde in 1976.*

of contra-rotating airscrews. The intention was to power the second prototype with Bristol Proteus turbo-props, which might have helped. As it was, the Brabazon was hopelessly under-powered. Its cruising speed was less than 250 mph and it required the Filton runway to be extended to 8,000 feet to get airborne, even at the commendably low speed of 85 knots.

It had two fundamental design weaknesses—the drag inseparable from a wing thick enough to stand up in, and major built-in fatigue characteristics, which soon became apparent.

Bill Pegg flew it over the Farnborough show in 1949 and 1950. It looked unbelievable. It was scrapped in 1952 following Duncan Sandys' pronouncement, as newly elected Minister of Supply, that 'Neither civil airlines nor fighting services could foresee any economic use for it.'

In fairness to the Brabazon Committee, their design recommendations also led to the de Havilland Dove, the Comet and the Airspeed Ambassador (later BEA's Elizabethan), all of which made their Farnborough debut by 1949.

It might be argued that the Brabazon Committee also sowed the seed of the Bristol 175 Britannia, which made its Farnborough debut three years later. It was powered by four Bristol Proteus turbo-props—the engines intended for the Brabazon II. Experience must at least have shown the Britannia's design team a number of pit-falls to avoid.

Bill Pegg was again the Chief Test Pilot in charge of the flight development programme. On an early sortie he survived the shattering experience of total power failure. He landed the prototype Britannia on a mud flat in the Severn Estuary. Thanks to his superb airmanship the only casualty was confidence in the Proteus, the retarded development of which had already spelt curtains to the Brabazon and indeed the Princess.

Now there was a sad story if ever there was one. The Saunders-Roe Princess made but one appearance at Farnborough, on the Tuesday of the 1952 show. The pilot was Geoffrey Tyson who, before the war, had gained the unusual distinction of flying the English Channel inverted in a Tiger Moth. He had further pursued this proclivity at Farnborough in 1948 in a long low-level inverted fly past in the only jet fighter flying-boat ever seen—the Saunders-Roe A1. Like the Brabazon it was an adventurous design, but simply not fast enough.

The Princess was not fast either, but she was certainly big, and beautiful beyond belief. The ten Proteus engines were built into the wings; the four inboard sets coupled to drive contra-rotating air-screws. With 25,000 hp rather than the design requirement for at least 35,000, she was grossly underpowered. It is said that Tyson's steeply banked low-level turn across the airfield was a great deal steeper and went on for much longer than he had in mind. The Princess was the world's biggest flying boat, ten tons heavier than the Brabazon, and larger than anything built in the USA, with the exception of Howard Hughes' Hercules which never rose more than 70 feet and that only once—and therefore, I suggest, cannot be properly called a 'flying' boat. The Princess also had the biggest pressurised hull ever built, twin decked and intended to accommodate 105 passengers in ocean-liner luxury. If that number of paying customers seems

small in relation to size, according to Neville Duke, BOAC were talking in 1946 of a trans-Atlantic supersonic airliner designed to carry *six* passengers and 1,000 lb of mail. The Comet originally went into service as a 36-seater, and the sums associated with Concorde's maximum of approximately 100 seats are all too familiar.

Why do British civil aircraft so often prove to be the wrong size to make money? Certainly BOAC were less than enthusiastic about the Princess, despite the fabulous pre-war tradition of the Imperial Airways Empire flying boats. George Strauss, Minister of Supply in the Attlee Government, had ordered three in the belief that 'Giant flying boats are essential in the long run for BOAC.' All three were built, cocooned, and the last one—the one we saw at Farnborough—was finally broken up in 1967.

In total contrast is the story of the world's biggest delta-wing aircraft, first seen at Farnborough on the same day as the Princess. The little Avro 707 research deltas seen in previous years had given us a preview. But who of those who saw it will ever forget their first glimpse of the second of Britain's V bombers, the mighty Avro 698—the Vulcan? When 'Roly' Falk flew it into the display it had logged just three hours. In a masterful touch of showmanship the huge white triangle appeared with a little 707 on either wing tip, one red, the other blue. People stood up and cheered.

The following year Avro staged a spectacular 'Delta Circus' with two Vulcans and four 707s, and in 1955 the Prime Minister, Sir Anthony Eden, concluded his visit to the show by leaving in a Vulcan. In his display the following day 'Roly' Falk trumped even that ace of one-upmanship. After pulling tighter and tighter turns at low level with the four Rolls Royce Avons in full cry, he levelled out to clear the control tower, on the roof of which I was standing. Then he heaved the nose up and rolled the Vulcan. I could not believe my eyes. The moisture squeezed from the startled air by that amazing manoeuvre actually fell on the control tower roof in a miniature shower of rain.

'Roly' never repeated this party piece at Farnborough, on whose instructions I know not. Years later, I told the story to Air Commodore Ray Davenport—himself a devoted Vulcan pilot—when we were broadcasting at the Battle of Britain Air

Left *Geoffrey Tyson flies inverted in the Saunders-Roe A1 jet fighter flying-boat.* **Opposite page** *Two more views of the mighty Avro Vulcan, seen here in 1962 fitted out as a flying test-bed for the Rolls Royce/Bristol Olympus engine for Concorde.*

Display at Finningley. 'It has been done elsewhere you know', he said. And there was such a twinkle in the eye of Air Commodore Operations at Strike Command that I had the distinct impression he was speaking from first hand experience. But do not quote me.

In 1958 a huge formation of Valiants, Victors and Vulcans from 10, 83 and 90 Squadrons roared low across Farnborough. The aircraft we had so recently marvelled at as prototypes presented a moving tribute to the designers and test pilots who had got them 'right' so swiftly, and into the hands of the front-line aircrews of the RAF.

Less glamorous, but no less successful was the Blackburn Universal Freighter, later named by the RAF the Beverley. It first appeared at Farnborough in 1950 and with a span of 162 feet was the second biggest aircraft then seen there. What is more, its pilot, Harold 'Timber' Wood, demonstrated that despite its size and unconventional shape, the Beverley enjoyed impressive STOL capability. The following year he became the first ever in the display to 'back her up a bit' after landing.

Another Big Beastie of outstanding excellence was the VC10, one of the world's first pressurised airliners to introduce a humidifier into its air-conditioning system. This was one of many factors which subsequently won it the preference of experienced North Atlantic passengers. Government funding was withdrawn after a mere handful were

*Above left The GAL 60 Universal Freighter which became the Beverley, photographed in 1950. **Below and left** British United and RAF VC10s—the former displaying its freight door to advantage. The latter photo was taken in 1966, at which time the aircraft was undoubtedly the most advanced—and best looking—airliner of its day. **Below right** A British United One-Eleven in 1964.*

built and forced upon BOAC. It made its debut in 1962 powered by four of the new Rolls Royce Conways which had attracted so much attention the previous year in the exhibition. With its smaller sister the BAC 111 (1964), the DH Trident (1962) and smaller still, the HS 125 (1962), Britain established the pattern for rear-engined high tail jets. The One-Eleven just missed the show of '62—Farnborough was henceforth bi-annual—and there was tragedy in its early story.

Engaged in high-speed stall testing on the One-Eleven prototype on October 22 1963, Mike Lithgow, who had contributed so much to Supermarine's early supersonic research, and his co-pilot Dicky Rymer, who had joined Vickers from BEA, were both killed. The aircraft fell out of the sky, wings level, nose high. Deeply grieved, Sir George Edwards halted further flight exploration of the problem until an emergency tail parachute could be devised which would induce a nose-down attitude to facilitate subsequent recovery. In his long and brilliant design and management career which ranged from the Wellington to Concorde, no setback had such a profound effect on Sir George as the loss of Mike and Dicky. I knew them both well enough to be certain that in no way would either have attributed the slightest element of blame to the design team headed by their friend and boss 'GRE', as Sir George was known to his staff. In the BEA Trident tragedy years later at Heathrow there were echoes of the same phenomenon. In that case it was induced accidentally. It was induced deliberately, and knowingly, by the two test pilots who gave their lives in pursuit of the safety of others.

A further tragedy at Farnborough must be recorded. On the Friday of the 1968 show I was watching from my commentary box high above 'The Hill'. The French maritime reconnaissance Breguet Atlantic appeared to me poorly placed for a spectacularly tight turn to land, particularly as one engine was feathered. To my horror I saw the wing drop and the aircraft instantly plunged into the old RFC hangars near the main gate. All five of the crew and an RAE employee were killed in the crash. The immediate fire was controlled with amazing speed by the ever vigilant Farnborough fire crews. New regulations concerning asymmetric flying during the Display were introduced forthwith. A cruel irony was that the Nimrod, BAC's super long range maritime reconnaissance jet was making its debut at the same show. Was the pilot of the Breguet trying too hard to defend the honour of France? I pose the question with every sympathy.

Amongst the most curious displays ever staged by the Heavy Brigade were those devised by another test pilot with whom it has been my good fortune to fly—'Slim' Sear. In 1959 and '60, he flew the Westminster, Westland's giant helicopter, with a steel girder of terrifying proportions dangling beneath him. With its naked lattice fuselage, the Westminster looked exactly the 'aerial crane' which the sales brochure claimed it to be. The following year, again flying the Westminster, 'Slim' went into the vehicle recovery business. He towed simultaneously down the runway at about 30 mph a Ferret armoured car, a one-ton Landrover and a transporter carying a Scout helicopter.

Not to be outdone, his colleague 'Sox' Hosegood, flying the Bristol 192 (now the Westland Belvedere) invited the 30 armed Royal Marines he had embarked to engage the crowd with their sub-machine guns. Subsequently the Commandoes 'abseiled' by rope to the ground—the first of many displays of this rapid method of deployment.

Left *The RAF's biggest 'beastie', the Short Belfast, photographed in 1964.*

Left and above right *Andover and Argosy. Although much more elegant than the American 'flying box-car' which it resembled, the Argosy was markedly less commercially successful.*

Right *A Hercules—successor to the Dakota as the work-horse of the Western world's air forces—at Farnborough in 1972.*

The Short Belfast was a 'Big Beastie' if ever there was one. The subject of major political controversy, it eventually appeared in 1964 powered by four Rolls Royce Tyne turbo-props. Attempts to arouse civil interest in its potential as a 300-seat airbus failed, but for 15 years it served with No 53 Squadron as the RAF's biggest weight-lifter with a maximum 34½-ton payload in its 84 foot-long freight hold.

Like the twin-boomed Armstrong Whitworth Argosy (Farnborough '56) and even the Andover (346 sold to date), the Belfast did not prove the world-beater transport its protagonists had hoped. The fears of the Brabazon Committee in 1942 have proved well founded. It is the all-American Lockheed Hercules which has become the RAF's Dakota.

Again the irony of world aviation is inescapable. The selection of the Rolls Royce RB211 for the Lockheed 1011 was the talking point of the Farnborough Exhibition in 1968. The airframe, the Tristar, brought the mighty Lockheed Corporation within an ace of financial ruin. We all know the RB211 story, carbon fibre and all that, and what

happened to Rolls Royce, entrusted by the Government in 1966 with a virtual monopoly of British aero engine design and production.

When the Tristar made its Farnborough debut in 1972 it provided an object lesson in applied PR. The Lockheed people could not have been more charming, hospitable and efficient. Like hundreds of others, I was offered, and accepted with alacrity, a ride in the Tristar. I knew it had a lift from the lower deck galley, and I entertained an impish ambition. Everyone has been trapped in a lift. But who has been trapped in a lift at 20,000 feet? I wasn't. The damn thing worked.

The sheer professionalism of that Lockheed operation reminded me of a story concerning another major figure in aviation whom I am proud to number amongst my friends—Air Chief Marshal Sir Denis (call me 'Splinters') Smallwood. When he was Commander-in-Chief at Strike, and also C-in-C NATO Forces UK, he was visited at his HQ at High Wycombe by HRH The Duke of Edinburgh. The Duke, piloting his helicopter to this appointment, did not enjoy the approach to land between high beech trees. He instantly expressed himself

on the subject in no uncertain terms, when greeted by his host. Closely studying a picture commemorating the event I said 'But Splinters, you are both wreathed in smiles.'

'That, my friend', he said, 'Is the smile of the tiger.'

Behind the story of the A300 European Airbus must lie many further examples of 'the smile of the tiger'. The British Government opted out of the project because the French, who had secured design-leadership, would not accept Rolls Royce RB211 engines. They rightly pointed out that at that time Rolls were unable or unwilling to meet the specification without delaying the project as a whole. Sir Arnold Hall of Hawker Siddeley decided to go it alone and totally without Government support secured the contract to design and manufacture the A300's advanced technology wing. It has gained the approbation of the world's leading aerodynamicists, and subsequently proved to be the vital pawn in the game when the Government belatedly attempted to make Britain a full partner in the 'Airbus Industrie' consortium. The story is well quoted by those who are uneasy about the possibility of miscalculation or political ineptitude when a country places its entire aircraft industry within the aegis of a single Government-controlled merger of hitherto independent companies. It is argued that only by the formation of such giants can the vast expense of contemporary and future development be met. But had British Aerospace then been formed and the industry nationalised, Sir Arnold and his board could not have exercised their own initiative when they considered the Government to have been wrong. Fortunately for us all, Britain is now a full member and Airbus Industrie proceeds from strength to strength to the benefit of its French, Dutch, Spanish and German partners, as well as providing this country with its only major stake in the big airliner business.

The beautiful and efficient European Airbus with American General Electric CF650 turbofans made its strikingly quiet debut at Farnborough in 1974. In 1979 it secured no less than 47 per cent of the world market for wide-bodied jets. Rolls Royce RB211s are now offered as an engine option and the Airbus has achieved at long last what the Brabazon Committee had in mind in 1942. ☐

Above *The Princess—beautiful beyond belief but hopelessly underpowered.*

Left *The famous low-level steep turn at Farnborough in 1953.*

Below *An early test-bed—the Tyne-Lincoln in 1956.*

Above right *Ambassador by Airspeed—first seen at Radlett in 1947 and still earning its keep for Decca at Farnborough in 1964.*

Right *Up-rated Ambassador with Rolls Royce Tyne turbo-props in place of the original Bristol Centaurus engines.*

Above and above right *The ill-fated Breguet Atlantic maritime patrol aircraft.*

Left and right *The HS 125 Series 700 executive jet—for the air-minded millionaire, charter or feeder line operator.*

Above *Farnborough backdrop for HS125 Series 700.* **Below** *The red, white and blue smoke trailed by the Red Arrows matches the patriotic livery on this BAC 111 Series 670.* **Opposite page** *The same aircraft 'living it up' over the manufacturers' chalets whose striped awnings are a hallmark of Farnborough hospitality.*

Opposite page *The Westland Westminster 'aerial crane' looking its part in 1959, less so in 1960.*

Above *A Bristol Belvedere completes an early example of helicopter tactical reinforcement capability.*

Above right and right *One of several 'last of the great bangers'—a Shackleton in 1952—and its successor in the maritime stakes, the Nimrod, clearly showing its Comet ancestry.*

Above left *Super VC10, once the connoisseur's choice for the Atlantic route.* **Below left** *An object lesson in PR—TriStar's debut in BEA livery.* **This page** *The world's most efficient sub-sonic wing in Farnborough fancy dress.*

Spin the Earth

Recording his own television obituary, Earl Mountbatten of Burma said 'In my experience men who are good at ceremonial are good at war.'

Like its comrade services the Royal Air Force proves Lord Louis' point, but with an added dimension. The Queen's Colour Squadron can match the Brigade of Guards on the Parade ground. The aviation equivalent of ceremonial drill has to be formation aerobatics. The Red Arrows and their predecessors have won the admiration of both the public and their peers. And the fighting capabilities of the RAF are proven.

I have been an unapologetic fan of the Red Arrows since Squadron Leader Ray Hanna moulded them into the team of self-disciplined artists which they are to this day. In itself that is remarkable. Despite the replacement of personnel necessitated by the passage of time and the accidental losses which could have broken a lesser team, the Red Arrows have preserved their standards of excellence since 1965. No other acrobatic team can match their record. True, the neat little Hawker Siddeley Gnat provided an aircraft admirably suited to the requirements of formation aerobatics. The Arrows have enjoyed opportunities undreamed of by their pre-war forbears. But the Gnat has its limitations, and one of the key factors in the Arrows' success has been their thoughtful exploitation of what it had to offer.

A highlight of pre-war RAF aerobatic displays was to tie together with ribbon the participant biplanes. Who would question that the Red Arrows' station-keeping is sufficiently accurate for them to be tied together? Having flown with them in display in 1969, with Tim Nelson when he was 'the boss', I can personally testify to the fact.

But apart from sheer speed (up to 400 + mph) and the problems of jet efflux, both of which would require ribbon of exceptional quality, to be tied together would deny the Red Arrows one of their salient skills. Their formations change constantly with such smoothness and precision that without the assistance of their own commentator, usually the team manager, the watching crowds would scarcely notice.

This again is typical of their professionalism. Since their purpose is to entertain those who come to watch, the Red Arrows soon realised that it was in everybody's interest to bring along their own man to tell the people what was going on.

That same professionalism dictates the immaculate appearance of their crimson Gnats, the distinctive overalls of pilots and ground crews, and their formation taxiing and parking, as well as take-offs and landings.

All this can be achieved only by the total commitment of every member of the team, on the ground as in the air.

Even so, the Red Arrows are remarkable.

One afternoon in 1966 Ray Hanna invited me to join them for a drink in the Farnborough Mess after the show. I pointed out that my 15-year-old son was with me. 'So?' said Ray, a devoted Dad himself; 'Bring him along.'

The approach to the No 1 mess-bar at Farnborough is along a corridor hung with portraits of the VCs of the RAF. What better introduction to the Service could any father have wished for his son?

Hot from their aircraft the Arrows were still wearing their crimson flying gear. After brief introductions Ray and I were soon deep in conversation about the show. I became aware that my son was no longer at my elbow. A quick glance revealed him at the bar, tankard (of shandy) in hand, engaged in happy chat with two of the team and their ladies—the prettiest girls in the room.

That these public idols should have had the kindness, as well as good manners, to 'See the

Opposite page *The Red Arrows' Gnats—something of which we can all be proud.*

The Red Arrows in 1968 with the red MGs loaned for their use at Displays by BMC's then Director of Motoring Publicity—their unapologetic fan.

young fellow right' with such easy and generous consideration speaks volumes. In one word—style.

In the air, the Red Arrows make it all look so easy that I sometimes wonder how many of those who watch think it is. In fact close formation aerobatics demand, as well as courage and a very high order of flying skill, total mutual confidence, and total concentration. The Arrows' full show lasts 14 minutes. During that time there is not a millisecond of respite for anyone, including the leader. Even the boxer has inter-round breaks, the golfer his walk from shot to shot, the tennis star the pause between rallies, and no soccer player is personally involved with the ball every second of the game. Only the grand-prix driver and the racing motorcyclist experience comparable demands on their conscious and subconscious reflexes. Perhaps that is why the Arrows have always enjoyed a close affinity with men like Graham Hill and Mike 'The Bike' Hailwood, both of whom flew with them.

That is a splendid experience. Only seen from the inside can the closeness of the Arrows' formation be truly appreciated during their big barrel rolls, at the top of their 'Join Up Loop', or in their eye-popping 'Twinkle Roll'. And do not think that all the leader has to do is fly around 'calling the shots'. His is the responsibility so to position himself that the Arrows are never out of sight of the main body of the crowd; that this hole in the cloud is exploited, that prohibited zone avoided, that the singletons are well-placed for their intersection passes—and throughout to fly the whole formation as smooth as silk, like one big aeroplane.

But the Arrows are the first to admit that they have learned from others. They inherited a great tradition. To name but a few, the nine tethered Hawker Furies of No 25 Squadron at Hendon in 1933, and four years later when the distinguished air correspondent 'Teddy' Donaldson was leading the Furies of No.1. In the late '50s and early '60s at Farnborough Treble One's 'Black Arrows' led by Roger Topp and Pete Latham, and the 'Blue Diamonds' of 92 Squadron—both with Hunters. In 1961 74 Squadron put up the RAF's first display team of supersonic aircraft—the Lightning. In 1963 56 Squadron were sensational with their nine Lightnings called 'The Firebirds'.

The Fleet Air Arm has certainly kept the White Ensign flying in the same context. Only the RN would call a formation team 'Fred's Five' and their display was the more impressive since they flew the big, heavy Sea Vixen. In 1958 Sea Hawks from No 800 Squadron and Scimitars from 803 did a synchronised display which proved more spectacular than intended. It included a 'live' ejection by Martin-Baker seat and the loss of one of the Sea Hawks—mercifully without casualty.

Also a major delight of innumerable air shows, including Farnborough, has been the display of the RN's Historic Flight—the gallant old Swordfish 'String Bag', the Fairey Firefly, and the Sea Fury—the last of the FAA's great 'bangers'. For many years the Fury was flown with typical dash and verve by Lieutenant Commander Pete Shepherd. He looks and plays the part, if ever an RN pilot did, and was the last 'Little Wings' aboard HMS *Ark Royal*.

The participation of the Fleet Air Arm at Farnborough has always been couched in terms disparate from those of the RAF.

In 1968 the Fleet Air Arm Aerobatic team consisted of six Sea Vixens from 892 Squadron. They produced a little six-page publicity brochure which included an enumeration of the five manoeuvres of their display: steep turn and loop in 'Broad Arrow'; change to 'Box 6'; barrel roll in 'Long Arrow'; loop in 'Spearhead'; bomb burst.

The Introduction, written by their then CO, Lieutenant Commander Simon Idiens, RN, requires no further comment.

'Due to operational and training commitments it is seldom possible to find time to practice the art of formation aerobatics. In February 1968, 892 Squadron disembarked from HMS *Hermes* to RNAS Yeovilton, having completed a full operational tour on board. We were reduced from twelve to six aircraft and given the task of working up an aerobatic team for displays throughout the summer, but, at the same time, to remain in operational training, which entails constant practice in such roles as rocketing, bombing and fighter interceptions.

'We were also reduced to six crews, three of whom were young aviators in their first squadron and none were hand-picked for the job. So we started from scratch, with average Naval fliers in a Naval front line squadron.

'It has been hard work, especially as the Vixen is a very large and heavy aircraft; we have learnt from our mistakes and the criticism of those on the ground (sic), but all of us agree that it has been an opportunity we would not liked to have missed.

'As Commanding Officer, I would like to pay tribute to the maintenance personnel, without whom all this could never happen. They are seldom seen, but work long hours to produce serviceable aircraft for us to fly.'

The brochure also included a portrait of their lion cub mascot (by courtesy of the *Daily Mirror*) and photographs of their wives.

All this may appear amateur by the standards even of 1968. It may also be of relevance to the Fleet Air Arm victories at Taranto and elsewhere. After all, no professional bunch of aviators could have taken seriously the suggestion to attack with the aircraft they had the pride of the Italian Navy in its own heavily defended home-base. Thank God for those gallant amateurs who did. But a heavier question mark must hang over the alleged 'professionals' whose lamentable failure to equip

Top right *A 92 Squadron Hunter in 1962. If the 'thin wing' supersonic Hunter design had not been abandoned, what might have been?* **Above right and right** *The Blue Diamonds in action in 1962.*

adequately the pilots of the Royal Navy committed them to such a fool's errand with aircraft which were obsolete by 1936. An apparent digression perhaps from what the Farnborough Air Display is all about. But is it?

Since Farnborough went international in 1964 we have also seen there formation display teams from overseas, notably the French 'Patrouille de France' (until 1953 the 'Patrouille d'Etampes') with their elegant butterfly-tailed Fouga Magisters, and the Italian 'Frecce Tricolori' with their beefy Fiat G91s. From both teams the Red Arrows have not been too proud to borrow a trick or two.

The RAF Free Fall Parachute Team 'The Falcons' have also introduced a new dimension into the art of aerial display. Using the human body as an airfoil, they 'track' across the sky at 120 mph. One party-piece is to link hands in a circle as they plummet down from 7,000 feet or more. Now that they are equipped with the 'flying wing' paravane their ultimate descent to the cross of the DZ is far more akin to formation flying than parachuting. On

many occasions successive team leaders have treated BBC Television viewers to flawlessly understated commentary by radio-microphone as the cameramen sought desperately to single him out from his converging comrades.

Rightly refusing to be up-staged by all this leaping about the sky, the Army has also displayed on many occasions at Farnborough. We have seen the 'Red Devils', the parachute team of the 14th Independent Parachute Brigade (a part-time group, unlike the Falcons and the Red Arrows), and the Army Air Corps' helicopter formation display 'The Blue Eagles', complete with travelling lady Adjutant.

But when it comes to helicopters, two achievements are outstanding. In 1972 test pilot Roy Moxam rolled a Lynx during the 'Westland Combine'. Today the Lynx roll is standard practice for RN display pilots although when first seen, like 'Roly' Falk's Vulcan roll, we blinked and wondered if our eyes had deceived us.

The other helicopter display to set new standards

Left and right *Fouga Magisters of the Patrouille de France in 1968.* **Above** *Eleven Magisters of the Patrouille de France commence their upward break in 1972.*

was flown by the German test pilot Siegfried Hoffman in the little Bölkow BO 105 in 1976 and '78. Several experienced test pilots told me they simply could not bear to watch, and not out of jealousy. Hoffman clearly entertained no doubts about his inability to break the four 32 foot diameter reinforced plastic blades of the unarticulated rotor system.

As to individual aerobatic displays at Farnborough, not a single year has lacked something remarkable. Mention of many has been made in previous chapters, and a definitive list would require a further book. But in the early 1950s Roland Beamont's Canberra bomber displays were brilliant by interceptor-fighter standards. More recently in '74 Irving L. Burrows' display in the all-American McDonnell Douglas F-15 Eagle was the talk of the show. It led to a curious prohibition against RAF pilots accepting demonstration flights in the F-15—a ruling so ill-judged as to smack more of Whitehall than HQ Strike Command.

Also memorable have been the displays of the Saab Draken and Viggen. Both big interceptors of striking appearance, their pilots have made maximum use of the power available—a single RR Avon built under licence for the Draken, and a Pratt & Whitney two-shaft turbofan developed in Sweden to give the Viggen Mach 2 performance.

Not lost upon the knowledgeable Farnborough crowds has been the scale of achievement by the manufacturers and the Royal Swedish Air Force, working as they do in isolation from the might of NATO or the industrial co-operation of the EEC.

Since a factor of Sweden's air defence philosophy has long been total dispersal, both these impressive aeroplanes are designed to operate off the long straight dirt roads of the Swedish forests if necessary, and accordingly have impressive STOL performance as well as the speed and handling of the missile dog-fight era.

The Anglo-French Sepecat Jaguar was the subject of much pre-flight publicity on the BAC stand in the Farnborough Exhibition. In our television show of 1968 we included a film-clip of its first flight within days of the event. But not until eight years later did we see a really impressive Jaguar display at Farnborough when the modification kit had been developed to coax more thrust from its twin Rolls Royce/Turbomeca Adours. I am not suggesting that the Jaguar was underpowered. But a few years ago when I visited an RAF airfield in Germany to make a short television film about Jaguars the trip was made memorable for two reasons. Firstly, it was a Heaven-sent opportunity to fly once again a front-line fighting aeroplane of the RAF. Secondly because the airfield was shared by a Buccaneer squadron, I saw appear on the notice-board in the Jaguar squadron's crew-room the following pointed message from their rivals: 'Jaguar pilots are requested to refrain from using reheat while taxiing past our dispersal. It frightens the cat.'

Also long awaited and much heralded in the Exhibition by those even remotely associated with the project was the Farnborough debut of the Multi Rôle Combat Aircraft—eventually named the Panavia Tornado. It first flew on August 14 1974, but not until the '76 show did it appear.

With so much depending upon its success, critical eyes were anxiously focused upon every second of its flight, and the initial response was frankly one of disappointment. It was not until Dave Eagles took over the display that the Tornado appeared the formidable advanced technology marvel it has to be if its commitments are to be met. It is, of course, totally false to judge the operational capability of an aircraft by the observation of a few minutes at an air show. Perhaps because of the standards long established at Farnborough its true importance may be over exaggerated. On the other hand there can be little doubt that to command respect and confidence from the public, let alone the experts, a new British aeroplane must be made to compare well in the display with those about it. Or questions will be asked.

Turning to civilian aerobatic displays, their many fans were delighted when the Rothmans Display Team were allowed to bring their Pitts Specials to

Below *The Rothmans Aerobatic Team of Pitts Specials—civilian rivals to the Red Arrows.*

Farnborough. Unfortunately we were never allowed to televise their classic display because of the BBC's curiously muddled policy concerning advertising.

A name well remembered by veterans of the early post-war period is that of Ranald Porteus. He used to do things with Auster variants that were a joy to watch. His successor in my submission would be Maurice Serret, Chief Test Pilot of Sud's Light Aviation Division at Toulouse. His entire display in various marks of the Rallye family has always been well within the Farnborough perimeter road, and his 'crazy' landings underline the necessity for total mastery in order to be funny in an aeroplane as elsewhere.

There has certainly never been anything funny about successive displays of the fabulous Britten-Norman Islanders and Trislanders. Apart from the precision of airmanship at low level, what made them remarkable was the sight of these amazingly successful feeder-airliners and maids-of-all-work standing alternately on their tails and noses, and generally behaving in a manner which could only be described as thoroughly skittish. No mere showing-off this, but an impressive demonstration of the aircrafts' ability to cope with anything the terrain or the weather might throw at them in those outlandish areas in which they have won a world-wide reputation.

In casting my mind back over 30 years at Farnborough I have been struck by, amongst many other things, a curious recurrence in the pattern of events, despite the huge strides of technical achievement. For example, in 1959 to demonstrate the Hunter's spin and recovery, Bill Bedford introduced the idea of 'making smoke' to trace his path. He executed a 13 turn spin drawing a vertical spiral in the Farnborough sky. In 1976 Andy Jones repeated the performance with the Hawk. Two years later the Hawk's European rival, the Marcel Dassault Alpha Jet, after, it is said, some measure of modification, proved that it too could recover from a multi-turn spin, in the hands of Jean-Marie Saget.

Maurice Serret suggested in his successive displays that it is virtually impossible to spin a Rallye. All embryo RAF pilots are taught to spin and recover. It is a pre-requisite for both man and machine. I sometimes wonder how much safer private pilots would be if it were possible for them all to be shown what really does happen if, in the words of John Farley, 'You break the rules about how the aeroplane works.' ☐

Right *Bill Bedford's famous 13-turn spin from 18,000 feet. Note the Hunter's vertical dive in the classic recovery position.*

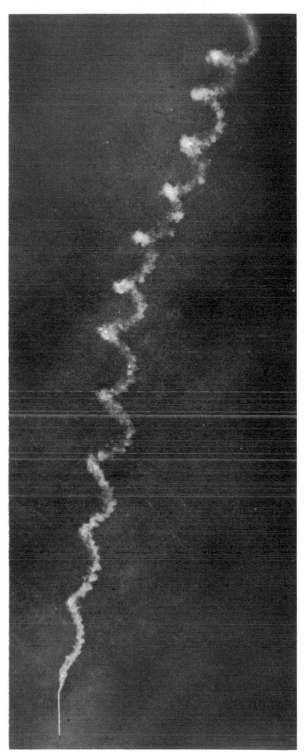

Left *Hawker Fury IIs of 25 Squadron.*

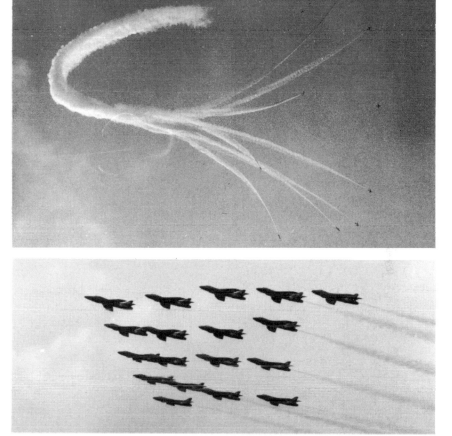

The Black Arrows. **Below left** *1958,* **above right** *1959,* **right** *1960,* **below** *1961.*

Left *Yellow before red—the Yellow Jacks ready for take-off in 1964 as the Vulcan clears.*

Below left *Nine Fiat G91s of the Frecce Tricolori barrel roll in 1972.*

Below *Scimitars in 1964.*

Opposite page *Two of the many important American Farnborough appearances in the late 1970s—the F-14 Tomcat and the F-15 Eagle, seen here in 1976 Bicentennial markings. A distinguished British test pilot said of the latter: 'He sits up there with perfect all-round visibility and performance to match, playing his computer like the mighty Wurlitzer, and believe me, it's impressive.' Was that why RAF pilots were forbidden to take a ride?*

Above left *Four of Fred's Five. Only the RN could have given that name to its display team!* **Below left** *Scimitar flypast at the 1959 display.* **Above** *A Fleet Air Arm formation display by Sea Hawks of 800 Squadron in 1958.* **Below** *A Scimitar in 1959 with 'thieving hook' at the ready.*

Above left *Jaguar under the ever-watchful eye of the emergency services, shimmering in the blast from the reheat.*

Far left and left '. . . a Heaven-sent opportunity to fly once again a front-line fighting aeroplane of the RAF.'

Above *High-speed peel-off by two of 74 Squadron's Lightnings.*

Right *74 Squadron's Lightnings in 1962.*

Above *Grass-clipping Jaguar at Farnborough . . . one can understand the Laarbruch Buccaneer pilots' request!* **Below and opposite page** *Airborne arsenals—the weapons options available to the Jaguar and Tornado.*

Sweden goes it alone—the Saab Draken in 1968 (left) *and the Viggen at the 1974 and 1976 Displays* (below left and above).

Right *Hawk familiarisation.*

Below *Marcel Dassault Alpha Jet in the static park.*

Left *Auster Alpine. 602 (Spitfire) Squadron had a 'supernumerary' Auster on its strength on VE-Day. The Station Commander told me to give as many rides as possible in it to the WAAFs and aircrewmen. So I did. Ranald Porteous flew Austers very much better than me.*

Below left *The Rallye family from Sud-Aviation Toulouse took over where Beagle left off.*

Above right *Always trying— Islander with Dowty fan in 1978.*

Right *The Trislander in 1974.*

Below *Conduct ill-becoming feeder airliners. The Islanders and Trislanders have always 'gone over the top' in the best theatrical sense at Farnborough.*

Overleaf *Scene from the air—a section of the 1978 static display.*